Class Warfare

Other Titles by William L. Fibkins

Angel Teachers: Educators Who Care about Troubled Teens

An Administrator's Guide to Better Teacher Mentoring, Second Edition

*Stopping the Brain Drain of Skilled Veteran Teachers:
Retaining and Valuing Their Hard-Won Experience*

Teen Obesity: How Schools Can Be the Number One Solution to the Problem

Innocence Denied: A Guide to Preventing Sexual Misconduct by Teachers and Coaches

Students in Trouble: Schools Can Help Before Failure

An Educator's Guide to Understanding the Personal Side of Students' Lives

An Administrator's Guide to Better Teacher Mentoring

Class Warfare

*Focus on "Good" Students
Is Ruining Schools*

William L. Fibkins

ROWMAN & LITTLEFIELD EDUCATION
A division of
ROWMAN & LITTLEFIELD PUBLISHERS, INC.
Lanham • New York • Toronto • Plymouth, UK

Published by Rowman & Littlefield Education
A division of Rowman & Littlefield Publishers, Inc.
A wholly owned subsidiary of The Rowman & Littlefield Publishing Group, Inc.
4501 Forbes Boulevard, Suite 200, Lanham, Maryland 20706
www.rowman.com

10 Thornbury Road, Plymouth PL6 7PP, United Kingdom

Copyright © 2013 by William L. Fibkins

All rights reserved. No part of this book may be reproduced in any form or by any electronic or mechanical means, including information storage and retrieval systems, without written permission from the publisher, except by a reviewer who may quote passages in a review.

British Library Cataloguing in Publication Information Available

Library of Congress Cataloging-in-Publication Data Available
ISBN 978-1-4758-0012-8 (cloth : alk. paper)—ISBN 978-1-4758-0013-5 (pbk. : alk. paper)—ISBN 978-1-4758-0014-2 (electronic)

∞™ The paper used in this publication meets the minimum requirements of American National Standard for Information Sciences Permanence of Paper for Printed Library Materials, ANSI/NISO Z39.48-1992.

Printed in the United States of America

Contents

Preface   vii

1   The Rise of Consumer-Driven Schooling: Fostering a Generation of Entitled Students   1

2   The Cost to Good News Kids and Parents   13

3   The Cost to Bad News Kids and Parents   29

4   The Cost to High School Principals   57

5   The Cost to Guidance Counselors   69

6   The Cost to Teachers   77

7   Schools Are Caught in a Bifurcation of American Society: Equal Opportunity Has Become a Forgotten Vision   83

References   91

About the Author   93

Preface

I wrote this book to raise the awareness of educators (particularly high school educators), parents, citizens, students, and political leaders about a bifurcation—a dividing into two parts or branches—of American society.

In our public schools, particularly in our high schools, we have two brands that are dividing our school community, educators, parents, and students into two parts. The college-bound and often affluent kids who are anointed as "special" and on the path to get ahead and stay ahead in the world I call "the good news kids" as they generate good news for their school that helps pass school budgets as well as bring ongoing prestige and accolades that send the message to the community that all is well and you should be proud to have such a wonderful school.

The good news kids are positioned to receive all the opportunities the school can provide such as expert college counseling, scholarship and financial information, connections to elite college admission officers, and the best teachers and classes. They are the best of the brightest, the standard-bearers, who seem more like a public-relations arm of the school administration than high school kids.

Their success is used by the school administration to market the school. In turn, they use the administration to garner the opportunities that will help them to get ahead and stay ahead, gathering the tokens of success that can be used to help them gain entrance into an elite college.

Yet they often seem old before their time. They seem polished adults, are seemingly the perfect children, and are never in trouble. That is, until the bottom falls out in their stressful lives, as I describe in chapter 2.

The other brand—I call them the "bad news kids"—often come from poorer families and have a long history of school failure, absenteeism, cutting classes, acting out in class, and suspensions. They are early on labeled as on the road to dropping out. They have little support, advocacy, or opportunity because they offer no good news to their school, only the bad news that comes with acting out problematic behavior.

Early on they learn they have no way to cross the bridge and become good news kids. Once in a while it may happen, but usually that path to becoming a good news kid is through athletic stardom. They have no token of success to help them cash in on a successful future. With luck they may graduate from high school, but in most cases they are headed for a menial job, the unemployment line, or military service because there are no other options available. Afghanistan beckons. Equal opportunity for every student, once a hallmark of the public schools after the civil rights battles, has now become a forgotten vision.

As Michael Sandel suggests (see chapter 1), we have become a market society, a society in which some students are valued more than others and are recognized as a brand, a commodity to be used as an instrument of gain and object of use by their parents and school leaders. As a result, good news kids and bad news kids do not share a common life with each other and rarely encounter each other in the course of everyday school life.

According to Sandel, students are treated as "instruments of gain" rather than as persons worthy of dignity and respect. This divide and isolation is seen not only in students but also in the separation of good news parents from bad news parents, elite teachers of good news kids from teachers of bad news kids, counselors for college-bound students from bad news kids in need of counseling, and overburdened high school principals from bad news kids and parents.

Robert Putnam (see chapter 7) argues that an inequality of opportunity among children is growing, and the future promises an America more divided than ever. Poorer kids have become more pessimistic and detached. Major institutions, including schools, but also family, friends, church, and community, have failed them. Many lack a sense of purpose and responsibility.

Columnist David Brooks (see chapter 7) suggests a long series of social and economic trends have merged to create this sad state of affairs. Traditional social norms have been abandoned and working-class jobs decimated. The result? Many middle- and lower-class parents are too stressed to have the energy or time to devote to their children. Meanwhile, more-affluent parents have invested much more in their children's future. Less-affluent parents have not, and the result is two brands of students in our schools: the good news kids who are blessed with opportunities, and the bad news kids who continue to litter the graveyard of failing kids.

The trend toward consumer-driven schools, which favors programs for get-ahead and stay-ahead students and parents, is propelled by strong forces led by affluent, politically savvy parents who demand the best for their good news kids.

David F. Labaree (see chapter 1), the author of *Someone Has to Fail: The Zero-Sum Game of Public Schooling*, suggests that consumers—the families who send children to school—want schools to accomplish goals that resonate personally; they want schools that help their children to get ahead and stay ahead. They are "families trying to fortify the future of their children through the medium of schooling."[1]

According to Labaree, "the vision of education as a private good (formed by the self-interested actions of individual consumers) has consistently won out over education as a public good (formed by the social aims of reform movements)."[2] This consumer-driven education model is focused more on credentialing than on learning, and the benefits flow to the good news kids. The bad news kids are relegated to a vocational curriculum which has a lower value. Schools are good at assigning labels that certify students at higher or lower levels of merit.

However, there is a dark side to this consumer-driven model not only for bad news kids and parents but also for good news kids and parents, high school principals, guidance counselors, teachers, and each school's mission to provide equal opportunity for every student. There is a cost being paid by every member of the school community.

This book's goal is to raise the awareness of educators, parents, students, citizens, and political leaders about this cost and its negative impact on equal opportunity in the schools. It is not an easy process to redirect, but it is one that will gain support if those involved see more clearly how bifurcation of our schools by consumer-driven schooling is damaging the mission of the schools to help each child be all he or she can be.

It's a story that needs telling if our schools are to be changed from being simply a brand for good news kids and parents. We need to remember that our schools are public. They are open to students from all walks of life and means. Citizens of all walks of life pay taxes and send their children to local schools, hoping to ensure a better future for them. Public schools are not private schools; they are not organized to serve only high-achieving students and parents.

NOTES

1. David F. Labaree, *Someone Has to Fail: The Zero-Sum Game of Public Schooling* (Cambridge, MA: Harvard University Press, 2010).
2. Labaree, *Someone Has to Fail*.

Chapter One

The Rise of Consumer-Driven Schooling: Fostering a Generation of Entitled Students

Times are tough. With budget cuts looming every year, administrators and union leaders find themselves in a never-ending game of proving how good their school is and explaining why budget cuts will derail their ongoing success. And the vehicle they choose for this ongoing self-promotion is what I call the "dazzle approach," which focuses only on good news, good news that can be easily translated into an ongoing selling campaign aimed at convincing school board members, parents, students, and community members that their school is performing at its highest level. The message is, Don't mess with success. Meaning, if you make drastic budget cuts, all hell is going to break out. Experienced teachers will be let go and replaced by inexperienced, untested new recruits. Chaos will become commonplace, and student bullying, failure, absenteeism, and dropouts will rise.

And where do educators find good news? In data about college acceptances, athletic and academic scholarships, winning sports teams, reduced behavior problems, increase in attendance, high-quality music and arts presentations, and community service programs that offer high-profile examples of students coming to the aid of citizens in the community. All this is fodder for the school's ongoing media efforts that say, "We are doing good, folks; vote yes on the school budget." The process is not unlike an elected politician who finds himself continually involved in promoting his electability.

But there is a costly dark side to this good-news-only process as it often results in caring schools and their staff abandoning their major focus on teaching/helping every student and turning their energy and mission into becoming a sales machine to pass budgets and survive. Over time administrators and staff often come to believe the positive reviews of the good-news process and overlook or abandon those students who don't make good news but instead act out, fail, cause trouble, and give the school a bad name. These are the "bad news kids," and their lives are not newsworthy.

They are the disenfranchised kids who have no real constituency in the school, labeled as "those" kids who don't participate in good-news programs such as sports, the arts, community service, and peer mediation. They don't make the honor roll, get their picture in the district newsletter, or receive accolades. Their name and the names of their parents make only one list in the school: the detention and suspension list. Result? The good-news-only process has the unexpected consequence of focusing too much on the best and brightest students who are the fodder for this good-news-only era. And, unfortunately, they are the students who get the most attention because they are the doers who drive the good-news process.

This process often yields a school community that operates in two different worlds with the bad news kids left to struggle at the margins of school life. This book is about the unintended consequences that can occur when the good-news process becomes deeply embedded in school life. It is about what can happen not only to struggling students who are seen as a handicap to selling the school's story but also to the best and brightest students whose successes are being used to sell the school's story—a process which creates two different worlds in a school community that prides itself on fostering unity and belonging.

The school media promotions may say "All is well here," but this positive spin belies the divisions that breed isolation and estrangement not only for the good news and bad news students but also for their parents, school administration, teachers, guidance counselors, and school/community discourse and engagement. One of the important lessons to be learned in this book is that too much dazzle, hype, and self-promotion can derail the real mission of the public schools: educating and guiding all students to be all they can be.

However, due to a bifurcation of American society, equal opportunity for every student has become a forgotten vision. There are powerful forces at work to manipulate our schools to widen the opportunity gap between college-bound, affluent kids who are anointed as "special" and on the path to get ahead and stay ahead and poorer kids who have little support, advocacy, or opportunity to get ahead. The marketing of these special students by leaders in the public schools, particularly high schools, is a prime example of this bifurcation, which results in yet one more thing to divide students, parents, and educators in the school community.

For example, the good news kids and parents are divided from the bad news kids and parents; principals are forced to use high-achieving students to sell their school's success and in the process become less involved with bad news kids and parents; teachers are called upon to pay more attention to good news kids to sell/tell the school's story and to pay less attention to bad news kids who have no good news to report; and guidance counselors are charged with developing good news data, such as college admissions, high test scores, rewards, and scholarships, in the process giving little attention to bad news kids.

Divisions are also orchestrated through the school's media presentations to community members which focus on only good news stories rather than giving an honest picture of the efforts by caring educators to bring success to every student. High schools used to be institutions that brought students and parents together from different walks of life to engage in a common project.

Unfortunately, those days are over in many high schools. Now the focus is on the best way to "sell" the school. And the chosen marketing tools to make the sell are the good news kids. As a result, these good news kids have become a brand in themselves, a commodity that is extremely useful in highlighting their school's "success" and in swaying taxpayers to vote yes at budget time. This is a process gaining great attention in these troubled economic times.

Michael J. Sandel suggests, "We have become a market society, a place where everything is up for sale. It is a way of life where market values govern every sphere of life."[1] It's a system in which some people are valued more than others; they are recognized as a commodity, as "instruments of gain and objects of use." And this system prevails in our high schools today.

Sandel suggests, "Democracy does not require perfect equality, but it does require that citizens share a common life. What matters is that people of different backgrounds and social positions encounter one another, and bump up against one another, in the course of everyday life. For this is how we learn to negotiate and abide our differences, and how we come to care for the common good and treat persons as worthy of dignity and respect, rather than as instruments of gain and objects of use."[2]

However, our high schools are not organized that way in our consumer-driven school world. Rather, we have a culture in which good news kids and parents are treated as "instruments of gain and objects of use." They do not share a common life with the bad news kids and parents. They do not "encounter one another, and bump up against one another, in the course of everyday [school and community] life."

Our high-achieving students are up for sale, not for money, but for the in-kind services they receive for promoting their school. For example, high-achieving students and their parents demand and get the guidance services they need to compete for admission to competitive colleges and to win awards and scholarships in return for waving the flag of success for their school and community. Graduation-day ceremonies for seniors are built around the achievements of these students, acknowledged by the superintendent of schools, whose speech highlights the good news of the numbers of students entering named colleges and their awards.

However, this good-news-only approach comes with a high cost that is often overlooked. The marketing of high-achieving students often results in a further separation and isolation of good news and bad news kids who, as Michael Sandel suggests, live increasingly separated lives in class-mixing institutions and public places that once forged a sense of common experiences and shared citizenship that now is becoming eroded. Opportunities for bad news kids and parents are also eroding with the creation of a school culture focused primarily on the marketing of high-achieving students.

In this good-news-only world, troubled teens need to look elsewhere for help. Many are not newsmakers whose activities and successes support their school's positive profile. They are simply kids looking for a caring, welcoming adult who can provide them with a trusting, safe place and help them forge a new plan for life. Their story is not a good-news story filled with many successes. However, it is a story they know needs changing with a hope for a new beginning. But for many, the help they need has eluded them so far.

This good-news-only process causes once-caring schools and their staff to abandon their major focus on helping kids and turn their energy and mission into becoming a sales machine for survival. Selling their school as a "product" becomes the number one priority. Over time, school administrators and staff come to believe what their public relations gurus are saying. They become smitten with these positive reviews rather than stay current in their classrooms. Often these schools take on an aura that they are Number One and that will never change.

However there is a real danger in focusing only on one's positive reviews. One gets to believe naively that only good things will continue to happen. This is a malady that also can affect educators in today's consumer-driven schools. As a result, administrators and staff begin to believe the constant hype, dazzle, and self-promotion and to deny the dark-side reality of their marginal students. In this process, they gradually lose focus on and interest in bad news kids and their stories. Their lives are not newsworthy. They are kids who live at the margins of the school and community life and who act out; fail courses; cause mischief and trouble; have alcohol, tobacco, and drug addictions; have poor health; suffer from eating disorders and obesity; and on and on. They are the disenfranchised kids who have no real constituency in the school.

They are labeled as "those kids" who choose to live as outsiders, loners. Their names and the names of their parents never appear in the good-news reports. That's only for the "other" kids. So hubris does its work and gradually sets the tone for the school and staff. There is so much effort and push by the staff to save themselves and their school that the process often has a negative impact on their classroom teaching. Unexpected consequences arrive.

Often it takes the form of settling, laziness, drifting, and abandoning the marginal kids who need their help, care, and energy the most. Sure, the school's ongoing public-relations "good news" reporting promotes a school that allows no child to fall through the cracks, but marginal kids and a few caring administrators and teachers know different. They know their school operates in two different worlds: one for the good news kids and one for the no-good-news kids.

As a result the process often alters the helping behaviors of once-caring teachers. They pretend they haven't changed and that they love and care for "all" their kids, but the school they once knew now exists in name only. The good-news process has become an unwanted visitor. It's now all about fame for the best and brightest, and these teachers are sucked up in the process, ready or not. Consciously or unconsciously using the good-news stories of the best and brightest students is the ticket to the survival of their school and themselves.

There are lessons to be learned from this consumer-driven schooling model. For example, be careful what you ask for. Self-promotion should be managed carefully. This is not an easy process. Schools and their staff do feel the real pressure to promote what they are doing. However, often in this process they oversell themselves. Result? In the process of selling their worth as a product, they, as the saying goes in sports, "Give up or ignore what brought them to the dance." What was a good school serving every student has now become a school focused solely on the good news students who deliver the positive spin that says, "All is well here."

Sandel calls this aspect of our market society the "skyboxification of American life," as exemplified by institutions such as the public schools where the achievers and non-achievers don't encounter one another in their everyday school life. They operate in two very different worlds and rarely come together as one to rebuild class-mixing institutions.

The good news students and parents are supported by a cadre of administrators, teachers, and counselors of the inner circle; the bad news students and parents operate at the margins of school life, looking in and often seeing no welcoming door for them. The good news students and their parents are seated in the skybox basking in their success, and the bad news students and parents are seated in the bleachers far from home plate.

No one is to blame for this isolating process, certainly not school administrators, teachers, and counselors, who are hard-pressed to pass school budgets and survive. They are victims as are the good news and bad news students and parents. Sandel suggests this marketing society is a result of Americans wanting more public services than they are willing to pay for and, in this case, of citizens wanting better schools but not wanting to pass school budgets and pay more taxes. This results in school leaders being forced to enlist their best and brightest students to hack and beg reluctant citizens to pass budgets and support their school.

This book examines the negative impact of the skyboxification of the public schools, in particular high schools, and their communities. School leaders often use the word "excellence" to describe their goal and identify their high-achievers as concrete examples that this goal is being met when budget times loom. However, as Charles J. Sykes suggests, there is probably no word used more frequently by educators than the word "excellence." They pledge it, commit to it, trumpet it, and include it in mission statements, press releases, curriculum guides, and endless presentations to parents, school boards, and local businesses.[3]

And this ongoing excellence sales campaign is often accompanied by a list of the standard-bearer students who are at the top of their class, winning numerous awards and honors, headed to elite or top-tier colleges. Sykes suggests the message to citizens is that these "excellent" students and their academic honors are worthy of the community's admiration and justify their support of the school district. The recent increase in bumper stickers reading "My Child Is an Honor Student at . . ." is an example of the growing marketing of honor students to endorse their school and present a pro-education message.

Sykes suggests these bumper-sticker messages are elitist. Not everyone makes the honor roll, which by definition excludes students who do not excel in academics. The peddling of honor students as picture posters for a school district's successful efforts to meet its "excellence" goals often results in a backlash, particularly among bad news students and parents.

Sykes offers the example of a July 1994 *Education Week* full-page commentary attacking these bumper stickers and lauding parents who had responded with a bumper sticker declaring "My Kids Beat Up Your Honor Student." The marketing of high-achieving students often brings with it resentment, jealousy, and feelings of unfairness not only toward these standard-bearers but also toward school leaders and parents who flaunt these academic feats.

Alfie Kohn suggests this process of selecting and sorting students so that only a few are recognized—via awards, weighted grades (which give an additional advantage to students in selective courses), honor rolls, and class rank—serves to distinguish one student from another. Kohn says it is a bumper sticker that says "My Child Is an Honor Student at . . ." (with the understood postscript, "And Yours Isn't").[4]

Kohn says this process raises the question of how we view education itself and refers to a book by David F. Labaree titled *How to Succeed in School without Really Learning*. Referencing Labaree, Kohn suggests "schooling these days is not seen as a way to create democratic citizens or even capable workers, but serves more as a credentialing mechanism. 'The purpose of education from this angle is not what it can do for democracy or the economy, but what it can do for me,' and this shift turns our school systems into a 'vast public subsidy for private ambition.'"[5] One implication of such transformation is that education becomes "an arena filled with self-interested actors seeking opportunities for gaining educational distinctions at the expense of others." This is precisely what we've seen affluent parents doing so relentlessly well.

Kohn also refers to Labaree's assertion that the point of education in today's world for students as consumers is not to get an education but to "get ahead and stay ahead." The process for high-achieving students unfortunately has evolved into an emphasis on massing credentials and marketing oneself by such means as developing relations with school leaders, and in turn the students are used to hack the excellence of school programs. Their reward for this relationship is receiving top priority from school guidance counselors to shepherd them into elite colleges.

It's a process built on a business model which says, "If you help me out in getting me into an Ivy League school, you can count on me and my parents to be your number one supporter and cheerleader." Maybe the process isn't so crass, business-like, or even conscious to many high-achieving students, but it is on the minds of many aggressive parents of the standard-bearers who, as Kohn suggests, weigh every decision about what their children do in school or even after school against a yardstick of what it might contribute to future success.

They are not raising a child so much as a living resume. Over time these often naive and hard-working students begin to be seen by school leaders, their parents, and themselves as "investments" in a marketing society and no longer as children enjoying school, hanging out, or having fun; they are seen now as a commodity to be sold to the community and to colleges making "the best offer," an offer their school leaders and parents post all over the school and community signaling "another example of excellence in our school and community."

For these students, everything has become about their future. As Kohn says, "The value of everything is solely a function of its contribution to the future, something that might come later. A process that will continue right through college, professional school, and right through the early stages of a career, until at last they wake up in a tastefully appointed bedroom to discover that their lives are mostly gone."[6] The parents of these high achievers have sacrificed their own children's present to the future.

These parents are living a life basking in reflected glory. And their children often live in fear of letting their parents down. Being a prized commodity also carries with it the intrinsic fear of many stars and celebrities, that one day your adoring fans may tire of you and leave and you'll be just an ordinary guy or gal. When the music and applause stops, it can be very painful to be alone on an empty stage.

David F. Labaree suggests in his book *Someone Has to Fail*, "This should come as no surprise. Because consumers—the families who send children to school . . . have wanted schools to allow them to accomplish goals that are . . . more resonant personally: to get ahead and stay ahead . . . In short, the vision of education as a private good (formed by the self interested actions of individual consumers) has consistently won out over education as a public good (formed by social aims of reform movements)."[7]

In this vision of schooling, Labaree says the benefits flow exclusively to the students who receive a particular level of education. And its value is that it offers these students an advantage in the competition for jobs that is not enjoyed by students who fail to receive the same quality of education. In this consumer-driven education model, the school system is focused on "credentialing" more than learning, and the benefits flow to the degree holder. Consumers are using their own interests through the schooling of their children to enhance their ability to forge ahead and stay ahead, or at least not fall behind, in a market society. And, of course, the good news kids are the ones most likely to get the credentials, diplomas, degrees, and jobs.

This consumer-driven school system is based on "What can it do for me?" and the "me" is the good news kid and his or her parents. As Labaree suggests, front and center is a consumer agenda for gaining benefits from schools to acquire marketable tokens of accomplishment. These include gold stars, high test scores, good grades, track placement, advanced placement, academic credits, and, most of all, diplomas.

And consumers in this market society are always on the march to acquire more marketable tokens for their children. For example, Donna St. George reports in "College Comes to High School," that there is "a growing interest in many areas of the country to go beyond work that is college-level and try college itself."[8] Experts say one goal of the courses is to blur the line between high school and higher education, with research showing that senior year, in particular, can be a dead zone of sorts for students who are done with most requirements but not yet onto the next challenge. Taking college courses ahead of time can keep them engaged.

Where does the pressure to acquire more and more marketable tokens end? And what is the cost to students who are always being asked to reach higher and higher and to their administrators, counselors, and teachers who must provide more and more marketable tokens to feed the appetite of parents who want to make sure their children get ahead and stay ahead?

Labaree says these costs are high as we find ourselves harnessed to the system we created, which continually spurs us to greater academic effort without ever letting us reach the finish line. The only way schooling can both let my child get ahead of yours and let yours get ahead of mine to constantly expand the system upward, which allows every increase in education access to be followed by an increase in education advantage.

The system is great at sorting students and giving them labels that certify higher or lower levels of merit. The good news kids have the advantage, and the bad news kids are on the outside looking in, not invited into the club or to the dance. They are spectators because they lack the marketable tokens required. The good news kids and their parents are the chosen ones in the organizational structure of the school system. The bad news kids and their parents are not part of this organizational structure, and their problems—lack of participation in the school dialogue, failure, poor grades, low test scores, poor attendance, discipline problems, dropping out of school, etc.—are not important to the school system because their poor performance doesn't affect the schooling in which the consumers, the good news parents and kids, own the advantage.

Certainly there is muted rhetoric, cries of concern for the bad news kids and their parents, such as PTA presidents lamenting the fact that "the parents who need it most don't come to our meetings" or guidance counselors wishing they had more time to "help these kids" instead of "just the cream of the crop," but everyone in the school community—students, parents, teachers, counselors, administrators, hallway monitors, custodians, etc.—knows the good news kids and their parents demand and get the resources to get ahead and stay ahead.

They have been given their marching orders, and the bad news kids are not a part of their mission. The bad news kids represent a distinct entity outside the consumer-driven organizational structure of the school. They have no educational currency, no marketable tokens such as gold stars, high test scores, good grades, track placement, advanced academic credits, and college-level courses.

The question this book asks is twofold: First, how can educators, parents, and community members intervene to give bad news kids and parents a new form of education currency so they can participate in the game of school, not be relegated to the bleachers of school life? Second, how can educators, parents, and community members intervene to reduce the ever-spiraling consumer-driven pressure on good news kids, parents, administrators, counselors, teachers, and citizens? It is a school world in which the good news kids and their parents are trapped by always being focused on the future and what comes next, while the bad news kids are trapped in a world which seldom offers them the necessary support and help to consider that they are entitled to a positive future, to their own dreams, and to feeling they have possibilities: to be in the club and have marketable tokens to get them into the dance of life, not peering in from the outside and feeling they will never belong.

Our work is to bring these two groups together and stop or at least reduce the isolation they are both experiencing. Can we assess the separation that has occurred in the school community without attempting an ill-advised effort to completely change our present consumer-driven schools? That's not going to happen. But we can, as this book hopes to do, become more aware of the dark side of the consumer-driven school world and consider a relatively small intervention that we can make to better understand and trust each other and to show we all have merit and belong as one to the school community. Kids trying to find their way should not be viewed as a commodity or as members of the chosen few. Instead, all should be following a path of exploration to futures that may be different, but have merit.

Our schools now require a major effort to develop a new form of education currency based on common respect, understanding, and acceptance. The present marketable token system may not go away, but it can be presented with a competitive model that can highlight a new path to follow.

NOTES

1. Michael J. Sandel, *What Money Can't Buy: The Moral Limits on Money* (New York: Farrar, Straus and Giroux, 2012), 202.

2. Sandel, *What Money Can't Buy*.

3. Charles J. Sykes, "No Rewards: The Attack on Excellence in America's Public Schools," http://my.execpc.com/-presswis/rewards.html (accessed June 6, 2012).

4. Alfie Kohn, "Only for *My* Kid: How Privileged Parents Undermine School Reform," http://www.alfiekohn.org/teaching/ofmk.htm (accessed November 6, 2012).

5. Kohn, "Only for *My* Kid."

6. Kohn, "Only for *My* Kid."

7. David F. Labaree, *Someone Has to Fail: The Zero-Sum Game of Public Schooling* (Cambridge, MA: Harvard University Press, 2010), 195–97, 217–18, 237, 243–44, 253–54.

8. Donna St. George, "College Comes to High School," http://www.washingtonpost.com/local/education/college-comes-to-high-school/2012/05/23/gJQAM8TrlU_story.html (accessed June 8, 2012).

Chapter Two

The Cost to Good News Kids and Parents

Good news kids are students who have been identified, anointed, to serve as standard-bearers to draw positive attention to their school. They have a long record of success dating back to elementary school days. They are students who have distinguished themselves over time for their leadership, high test scores and grades, and involvement in many extracurricular activities and community service. They are students whose achievements are regularly reported in local and area newspapers and media as well as the school's public-relations outreach to parents and citizens.

They are also regularly asked to speak at community organizations such as the Lions Club, Kiwanis, Veterans of Foreign Wars, and local charity groups as part of their fundraising activities. They are poster children for their school's success. They are somebody of importance on their school campus, and as such they carry with them the need to be a model student; that is, they must be well-behaved, have good attendance, show no acting out behaviors, and be kind and accepting of their peers. In their leadership role these standard-bearers are the messengers of good news to the school and community, and in particular to a voting public that can pass or vote down yearly school budgets.

This is a much-sought-after role, and at face value it seems like an honor filled with many rewards that may help them to get into a "name" college, which is the dream of every high-achieving student and parent. But the role has a dark side that is often unseen by students who become standard-bearers and their parents. For example, accepting this role is like signing a contract with the school that you will carry the flag to promote your school, the good news, and, more subtly, yourself. It's a full-time sales job to be seen and heard at many school and community venues, to tell members of the school and community that "all is well . . . look at my success . . . the school, my teachers made me what I am today."

It's also a role in which students can be used to hack a school's success, serving devotedly as minions, a role that seems exciting at first but over time raises the question for students, "What's in it for me?" And, often, the answer is, "Getting into a good college." Students find out being "somebody" and "famous" in their school and community can be tiresome, hard work, and no fun. They have come too fast into an adult world that is serious business, with much at stake politically for their school. They have become key players to help lead this political battle to put a happy face on their school and pass the school budget. Their reward, as promised, will come when their letter for college acceptance arrives. But some wonder, is it worth it to be a "somebody" and carry the flag of success for my school? There are costs.

And the dark side includes being estranged from many of their fellow students, who now begin to view these students as "different." And they are "different" because they now are totally engaged in studies and leadership activities, and they now travel in adult circles with teachers, administrators, school board members, political and community leaders, and media personnel following "their" story. Stories help sell newspapers. Everyone likes a winner and an example of home-grown success. Peers pick up on this "differentness" early on and stay away. They are involved in their own teen world of hanging out, partying, dating, learning about sex and life, and just being kids. They know that someday soon they will have to enter the adult world, but not now.

The dark side also includes the wrath of the bad news kids who operate at the margins of school life and are often in trouble for acting out, doing drugs, smoking, drinking alcohol, fighting, and failing courses. These are the students who give their school a bad name and are known in the school and community as "losers," the ones who regularly provide fodder for community groups critical of the school and anxious to defeat school budgets. These students often see the standard-bearers as too good. They see them as pets of the school administration and teachers who always seem to be truckling to them and heaping praise on their achievements. The bad news kids often come to school angry, and there is no better target for them to express their anger than good news kids who play by the rules even when it costs them.

This dark side then creates a role, the "perfect kid" role, in which the standard-bearers are unable to choose an imperfect school and home life or to act out, to be "bad boys or girls." They cannot choose a world in which they would be able to fail, falter, miss assignments, skip school, oversleep, be late for class, punch out a classmate for name-calling, be suspended and serve detention, or not be on the list of teachers and school principal as a "favorite" student. Rather, these star students are always on their best behavior and daily don the cloak of perfection. These are often kids who became adults too soon and lose their childhood along the way.

Being the perfect kid can be a trap for life. High school students who attempt to exit this role face many barriers from their parents, teachers, administrators, and even their peers. The perfect kid is a known quantity and depended upon by the entire school community. He or she provides a steady, positive presence in a turbulent, often chaotic, school world. These high achievers know that if they tell their parents, teachers, administrators, and peers that they "want out," the prison gates of their star world will slam shut.

Parents, the school, and the community understand the importance of these star students, and they will offer great resistance to losing their poster child. Like champion horses, these students are being ridden to demonstrate to the school community that the school is developing home-grown winners. There is no easy way out of this good-news role for these chosen students. But for some, they keep their fears and concerns hidden until it's too late. Their role, as it has always been, remains one of keeping everyone in their lives happy: parents, teachers, administrators, peers, and community members. Early on they learn to put on a happy face and never show others their true feelings. That's what good news kids do.

As a result, some seek relief from the pressures involved in this role through self-destructive involvement with alcohol and drugs. And when the bottom begins to really fall out in their young lives, suicide sometimes becomes an option. All is not well in the world of today's valedictorians and salutatorians. Here's an unnerving picture of what we have wrought in marketing our high-achieving students and their schools as a "success" to consumer-driven voters.

Alan Schwarz, in his article "Risky Rise of the Good-Grade Pill," describes a world in which star high school students are increasingly abusing prescription stimulants due to pressure of grades and competition for college.[1] Pills that have been a staple in some college and graduate-school circles are going from rare to routine in many academically competitive high schools where teenagers say they get them from their friends, buy them from student dealers, or fake symptoms to get prescriptions from doctors.

For example, Adderall, an amphetamine prescribed for Attention Deficit Hyperactivity Disorder (ADHD), is being used by students in affluent suburbs of New York City and elsewhere in order to study late into the night, focus during tests, and ultimately get the grades worthy of their prestigious high schools. Schwarz says the drug does more than just jolt them awake for an eight a.m. SAT—it gives them a tunnel focus tailor-made for the marathon of tests known to make or break college applications. A student at one school reports, "Everyone in school either has a prescription or has a friend who does."

In his research for the article, Schwarz contacted more than two hundred students, school officials, parents, and others. About forty agreed to share their experiences. Most students spoke on the condition that they be identified by only a first or middle name, or not at all, out of concern for their college prospects or their school system's reputation and their own.

As Schwarz reports in his interview with a student identified as Madeline, the main goal of these high-achieving students is keeping everyone happy. Here's Madeline's story. It may be a good-news story for her parents, teachers, and principal, but it's not a good-news story for her.

> Madeline surveyed her schedule of five Advanced Placement classes, field hockey and several other extracurricular activities and knew she could not handle it all. The first physics test of the year—inclines, friction, drag—loomed ominously over her college prospects. A star senior at her Roman Catholic school in Bethesda, Md., Madeline knew a friend whose grades had gone from B's to A's after being prescribed Ritalin, so she asked her for a pill.
>
> She got a 95. Thereafter, Madeleine recalled, she got Adderall and Vyvanse capsules the rest of the year from various classmates, not in exchange for money, she said, but for tutoring them in calculus or proofreading their English papers.
>
> "Can I get a drink of water?" Madeleine said she would ask the teacher in one class, before excusing herself and heading to the water fountain. Making sure no one was watching, she would remove a 40-milligram Vyvanse capsule from her purse and swallow it. After 30 minutes, the buzz began, she said: laser focus, instant recall and fortitude to crush any test in her path.
>
> "People would have never looked at me and though I used drugs like that—I wasn't that kid," said Madeleine, who has just completed her freshman year at an Ivy League college and continues to use stimulants occasionally. "It wasn't that hard of a decision. Did I want only four hours of sleep and be a

mess, and then underperform on the test and then in field hockey? Or make the teachers happy and the coach happy and get good grades, get into a good college, and make my parents happy?"

Madeleine estimated that one-third of her classmates at her small school, most of whom she knew well, used stimulants without a prescription to boost their scholastic performance. Many students across the United States made similar estimates for their schools, all of them emphasizing that the drugs were used not to get high, but mostly by conscientious students to work harder and meet ever-rising academic expectations.

Schwarz also reports,

> Douglas Young, a spokesman for the Lower Merion School District outside of Philadelphia, said prescription stimulant abuse was covered in various student-wellness indicatives as well as in the 10th-grade health curriculum. Mr. Young expressed frustration that many parents seem oblivious to the problem. "It's time for a serious wake-up call," Mr. Young said. "Straight A's and high SAT scores look great on paper, but they aren't reflective measures of a student's health and well-being. We need to better understand the pressures and temptations, and ultimately we need to embrace new definitions of student success. For many families and communities, that's simply not happening."

It certainly was not happening for Madeleine, who suggests, "Isn't it better to take a pill and make the teachers happy and the coach happy and get good grades, get into a good college and make my parents happy?" Schwarz says, "One consensus was clear: users were becoming more common . . . and some students who would rather not take drugs would be compelled to join them because of the competition over class rank and colleges' interest."

While Douglas Young is right on when he says we need a new definition of success, the everyday reality in his school and many consumer-driven high schools remains entrenched in a culture that says to star students, "Do whatever you can to get ahead and stay ahead and in the process champion your school's success."

Schwarz provides an example of how students view their consumer-driven school world for what it is. Their analysis and observations should serve to warn school administrators like Mr. Young that they are part of the problem not the solution. They are a major part of a school culture that embraces the "get-ahead, stay-ahead," consumer-driven race to the top. Offering a variety of initiatives on the abuse of stimulants is a nice idea, but it does little to curtail the constant pressure on the best and brightest students to succeed. When a swimmer is in rough, turbulent waters and fears going under, he or she will grasp any kind of a lifeline. Same for high-achieving students who feel they are sinking into a poor performance funk.

Here's some advice for Douglas Young, his peers, and the parents of his best and brightest students from an Alan Schwarz article, "In Their Own Words: 'Study Drugs,'" that offers some beginning paths to a solution.[2]

Mary, twenty, from Los Angeles says,

> Let me say first off that I take full responsibility in choosing to take Adderall as a study drug. It definitely helped me get good grades during finals, but plenty of students get good grades without it, and I would understand if somebody in my classes felt cheated because I took it.
>
> That being said, the immense pressure put on students by parents and educators has made taking speed a socially acceptable thing. I come from a family that gets disappointed and chews me out for B's or even B+ grades and A-'s. My whole life I've been told that, no matter how smart I am, the only way to be successful (see: acceptable) is through academic excellence. Now, would my parents be upset that I've taken study drugs? Probably, and that's just symptomatic of the problem.
>
> I'm sick of the expectation of a "perfect" kid. The parents and educators in this article who express shock at kids using study drugs ought to look in the mirror; they are equally responsible. College is harder to get into today than it was and it is much more stressful and difficult once you get in. Change your unrealistic expectations or take the My Kid is an Honor Student bumper sticker off your minivan.

This assessment provide a clearer and much needed picture of the cost to high-achieving students who find themselves thrust into a "star" role as young children and adolescents. "

Judith Warner supports Schwarz's argument about the rise of stimulants among high-achieving high school students.[3] Warner says the widespread use of stimulants like Ritalin and Adderall by teenagers is a problem that has been created as much by adults as by young people who actively engage in the illegal use and trade of drugs. It has been fostered by an adult-stoked environment of extreme competition and near-hysteria over the perceived super-human effort required to gain entry into a prestigious college.

Warner suggests that if adults really want to combat the problem, they'll need to start confronting their own attitudes and behaviors. Parents need to push back against excessive pressures and reorient their kids toward more meaningful and healthy notions of success.

She urges "less pressure to be a star student, more conversations about the risks of using stimulants as a performance drug."

The following vignette, "The Advanced Placement Courses Can Kill You,"[4] is about a star student who was searching for relief from too many pressure courses and who might have been close to abusing stimulants or, worse, contemplating suicide. This is an example of the kind of conversation that Warner suggests is needed between star students and their parents before the bottom falls out of their lives. It is a conversation that changed the life of this particular star student for the better and vividly portrays how hard it is to be a "perfect kid."

> I was the standard bearer. You know, the one child in the family who is supposed to do well after all your older brothers and sisters have screwed up. I knew my parents were depending on me to get into an Ivy League college and get a scholarship. It had always been that way. It was "the way" that had been chosen for me since I was selected to be in the gifted and talented class in Grade 6. It was expected. I remember hating the gifted and talented class.
>
> I hated being taken out of my regular classes, especially gym. The gifted class met on Tuesday and Thursday and those were my gym days. So I hardly played gym in junior high. And I used to hate what the other kids said about me when I left the room for the gifted class. They would say, "There goes the nerd" and "It's just us dumb ones left now." These were kids I had grown up and gone through school with.
>
> Now, suddenly, I was different. I was no longer one of the guys. I was being shipped out to a special room where we did these experiments and talked about philosophy. I hated it but I knew my parents were proud of me and it made them important. I was the last of four kids and all the others had really screwed up in school. Somehow, when I look back, my being in the gifted class made everything all right with my parents. They weren't failures after all. So I tried to block out all the comments from other kids and do my best.
>
> I knew that someday, once I got through all this school stuff, I would be able to do what I wanted to do. But that would have to wait. So I went along. Each year I won the prize for the highest grades. It came pretty easy, particularly in junior high and in Grades 9 and 10. Each year I was picked to attend a special gifted and talented program at some ritzy school like Andover. My dad saved all my newspaper

clippings and honors; he said, "All of this stuff is going to look great on your college applications. Believe me when I tell you all this work will pay off." The folder with all my stuff grew and grew. I was "somebody" in my town.

People were proud of my success. Wherever I went, the parents and townspeople would ask, "What Ivy League school are you going to?" Some schools had winning football teams to be proud of. In our town it seemed to me that people put all their pride in me. I was on my way to something really important, and it made my parents, my school, and my town feel better about themselves.

But then it happened! I hadn't wanted to take the four Advance Placement courses in my senior year. It seemed like too much. I wondered why I needed all those courses. I had taken every difficult course offered in the high school and special programs in the summer. Even now I was taking two advanced science courses at the community college at night. I thought enough is enough. But my parents and some of the teachers insisted that these courses would make me a "shoo-in" for the Harvards and the Yales. It would put the icing on the cake. There was no saying no because I had never said no before. The words "I would like" and "No, that's not for me" had never come out of my mouth.

I was the good child who always took on more than I had to. I was the standard-bearer who had to do well. So I took the English, math, and two science AP courses. After all, it was my senior year, only nine months to go to graduation. I could handle it. But before long I realized that I couldn't keep up. I had all the AP courses, college applications and visits, my night courses, and preparing for the SAT exams! It became a nightmare. I had no time to myself and every course was tough. I couldn't cut myself any slack. There was no time in the day to hang out and hear my music. Plus everyone expected me not just to do well but to do very well in each course.

I was like a star fullback who was being given the ball on each play. I couldn't keep up. The first sign was that I started shaking; I would literally be twitching twenty-four hours a day. I couldn't stop my eyes and arms and legs from "jumping." And then I began to lose weight. I couldn't relax and I couldn't eat. On top of all that I couldn't sleep and I had awful nightmares. I found myself unable to do my homework. I couldn't believe this was me. It was almost as if I were caught in some crazy plot to keep myself from getting into an Ivy League school. If this kept up, I feared I would end up at a state school or, worse, a community college.

I tried to shake it off but instead found myself cutting classes and leaving school early. I was so confused and embarrassed! Everyone was looking at me like I had become a weirdo, I was shaking all the time, and the teachers kept asking me if everything was all right. Even my dad sensed I was in trouble. One night I came home from community college and found my dad in my room writing out "my" college applications. I yelled at him (the first time in my life), "What are you doing? That's my job." He said, "You look under pressure; I was just trying to help you. I didn't know what else to do."

I started to cry so hard that I couldn't stop. I remember saying, "Dad, I can't do all of this anymore. I'm over my head. I never have time to play or hang out. I've always, always studied and worked at school. I can't do it anymore. I don't know why but I know I can't. I can't stop shaking; you've seen me, look at me now! And I can't eat or sleep or do my homework.

"All the kids and teachers at school look at me like I'm going nuts and I think I am. All I know is that I have to drop the AP courses and the courses at the community college or I'm going to crack. And I don't want to crack. Dad, I'm not asking you, I'm telling you that it has to be that way. I may be letting you and Mom and the school down but I want to have a normal life like the other kids. I've never hung out or had a summer where I had a job and went to the beach. I've never had time to even have a girlfriend. I know other kids and their parents look at me and think, 'He's got it made.' But look at me, Dad, I can't do it anymore!"

Dad sat there stunned. It must have been twenty minutes before he came over and put his arms around me and said, "Maybe we've made a big mistake. We had so much trouble and pain with the other kids that when you came along and did so well, it made everything easier for us. We didn't have to be ashamed every time we went into the school. We didn't have to worry when we heard the police siren. We didn't have to worry about you coming home drunk or high on the weekends. Because of you, your Mom and I became somebody decent in the community after all the years people said things about how terrible our kids are. I knew you'd never be in the DWI column in the paper.

"But maybe we did put too much pressure on you. God, I'm so sorry for doing it to you. I never thought we were hurting you but now I see it was all too much." He was crying, we were both crying. He said, "It's not too late. We'll go to the school tomorrow and drop those courses. You probably have more credits than anyone in the state anyway. You can take regular English and whatever else is required. And you can drop the night courses. Why the hell did we make you do all of this? It was crazy. As for the applications maybe you should write your essays about all of this. What would we call it? 'Almost Burnt Out by Eighteen?' When your Mom gets home we'll tell her that you've decided to make some changes. It looks like you need to do a little less gifted and a little more fun. I love you."

So, my life changed. All the kids and teachers were surprised when I dropped the courses but they knew I had had enough. Some people spread the rumor that I had a "nervous breakdown." Maybe I had. But my life had changed for the better. I still got into some Ivy League schools but I am postponing that, going slow and taking courses at a community college. I know now that I'll be okay. I guess in some way I can thank the AP courses. I wouldn't have had my "problem" if I hadn't let my parents and teachers (and myself) push me into those courses. Maybe now I can make my own decisions because I know what can happen if I don't. I never want to feel that way again.

One of the lessons in this vignette is that perfectionism in high-achieving students can have its cost. Perfectionism creates great difficulties for gifted students. It's often caused by a long history of As in school and the continued glowing feedback from parents and teachers. The children become dependent on this continuous praise for their self-definition and feel strong pressure at a level that matches the praise.

There may also be family pressures and self-pressures for "perfect" work that cause high-achieving students to expect perfection in all areas. If they do less than perfect, they feel like failures. Some spend their lives worrying, feeling guilty, and working hard. Their identity is at stake, and they work desperately to protect it. Perfectionism is a heavy burden for star students, so we should not be surprised if and when they turn to a "little help from their friends" such as stimulants to ease the pressure.

As the student from Los Angeles described in Schwarz's article suggests, "I come from a family that gets disappointed and chews me out for B's or even B+'s and A-'s . . . I'm sick of the expectation of a 'perfect' kid."

Some of these "perfect" students are like a bottle of beer left out in a boiling-hot sun. At some point it's going to explode and can't be put back together again. There are "danger points" for high-achieving students trapped in the role of serving as a minion for their school and community.

But who's watching for them to explode, falter, and want out of the race when the track gets steeper and steeper? For them, to say "I'm done, I am getting out" is not so easy. Someone needs to hear their cry and act to help them. Warner suggests we need more conversations about how to lessen pressure on star students. But is the school culture really interested in doing this, given that it is a consumer-driven organization that is dependent on using these star students to woo the support of voters by generating a constant barrage of good news?

It appears that school administrators, counselors, and teachers are also trapped in this good-news-only culture which makes it difficult for them to notice, hear, and respond to danger points that impact star students and which are diminishing their role in serving to meet the needs of every student. It is difficult for successful educators to stop reading the reviews of how wonderful they and their schools are. For them the show must go on, and the star students are the main actors, dancers, and chorus line all wrapped in one. The role of successful educators is to serve as choreographers for this good-news-only show. Where would they be without their good-news troupers?

Instituting efforts to put less pressure on star students can be a risky task for educators who are leaders of a get-ahead, stay-ahead, consumer-driven organization. That effort would require an honest assessment of the impact of excessive school pressures on these students' health and well-being, an assessment such as Schwarz's that exposes students' search for relief through stimulants, drugs, and other self-destructive behaviors and also the attitudes and behaviors of the school administrations, counselors, teachers, and parents who have supported this kind of school culture. As a male student from Los Angeles suggests, "The parents and educators . . . who express shock at kids using study drugs ought to look in the mirror; they are equally responsible."

However, any effort by some educators and parents to reorient students toward more meaningful and healthy notions of success will surely be met with strong resistance from the get-ahead, stay-ahead crowd who dominate school life. Douglas Young of the Lower Merion School District is spot on when he suggests, "We need to better understand the pressures and temptations, and ultimately we need to embrace new definitions of student success. For many families and communities, that's simply not happening." However he is probably one of the few education leaders to take this stand. Implementing change is often a lonely, uphill battle, and a battle that can include the loss of one's job. When Young suggests, "For many families and communities, that's simply not happening," he might add, "For many educators that's simply not happening."

Are our schools and communities ready to admit the dark side of the pressures on our star students and try to find the alternatives to consumer-driven schooling that Douglas Young is asking for? The answer is, probably not, given the reality that, in our consumer-driven schools, star students are seen as commodities, as "instruments of gain and objects of use," as consumer goods. These star students are not children worthy of respect and dignity because of who they are as individuals, but rather they are children like Madeline in Schwarz's article who are raised to be minions and servile followers and to keep everyone—parents, teachers, coaches—happy. They are teenagers who find themselves living in an adult world. They know they are different.

There has been too little discussion in our schools and community about the valuing, health, and well-being of star students. It's a story that never reaches the front page. Yet, it's a story that everyone in the school community knows exists, but there is little will and too much fear to engage the school community in such a discussion. As in any other human-relations problem, people tend to stay fixed in the world they know, no matter how problematic. They don't ask whether star students are "goods" that are valued more highly and are more worthy than other students, why this is so, or how this valuing might be changed. As some educators say, "It is the way it is, don't make waves." Douglas Young says, "We need to better understand the pressures and temptations, and ultimately we need to embrace new definitions of student success," but he is among the minority who are trying to raise the awareness of teachers, counselors, parents, administrators, and community members. It's a risky, courageous move for Doug Young and his career and job safety.

This discussion, or the thought of it, tends to make many parents, teachers, counselors, and administrators uncomfortable because it removes the fantasy about the "All-American," perfect kid—the star student who is a leader, strong, smart, compassionate, honest, honorable, caring, wise beyond his or her age, and pure. This star student has no dark side or problems. He or she is everyone's friend, protector, hero, and model to follow, a Hollywood story that is taking place right in their own school and community.

Parents of star students in particular will avoid this discussion because they are intertwined with their child's success, fame, and fortune. They hang on to their own star role until it comes to a crashing halt the day after the graduation celebration. Then star students and star parents suddenly lose their status as "instruments of gain and objects of use." They are stripped of worth, their role in the school-community hierarchy; they are no longer in the club and valued. No, they don't receive a call, an e-mail, or a letter announcing their exit, but it's a done deal. The applause that once greeted them at PTA meetings dies fast. They were once a "somebody," but now that the graduation stage has been emptied, they are a "nobody."

Don't bother telling this to parents of star students. They won't listen. They are too busy basking in the success of their child, seemingly oblivious to the rigor of the role. That is, until the star student hits a roadblock, falters, and is sent to an outside-of-school psychologist (not a school counselor who might let the principal and key educators know the kid is troubled) who can discreetly get the star student back on track quickly.

With help, the star student and his high-achieving peers finally jump through enough hoops—e.g., PSAT, SAT Advance Placement courses, selection for the Honor Society, being voted most likely to succeed, college applications and interviews—and are lauded at graduation ceremonies, are rewarded with a diploma, gain entrance into an elite college, and are profiled in the local newspaper as the best and brightest our fine schools are turning out. "Home Grown and Proud of It," might be the headline of the profile.

Of course, the parents are proud. There are lots of pictures and newspaper clippings for relatives and friends, and there is ordering of college sweatshirts and caps, making reservations to travel for orientation, and buying a new and very preppy wardrobe so the student will blend in as one of the in crowd, including the latest laptop and cell phone so he or she is seen as up to date—a winner.

But after a few weeks the hype and dazzle of graduation week stops. The star student is no longer a "somebody" in his community. He's simply a kid going to college. Sure, everyone wishes him luck, but his value as a commodity to his school and community is over. He is an empty suit, no longer a "someone" who turns heads in school, and he is not yet a student in a college miles, hours, maybe days away.

For the first time in his career he is no longer a "somebody." His honors, diploma, yearbook, accolades, and testimonials to his greatness have been put away in a trunk to be remembered sometime in the future, when his parents show them to his children and recall what a smart student and great guy their dad was. He will soon begin college as one of many newcomers with dazzling resumes who are also no longer "somebody," and this college will be a place where no one cares what you did before, but rather what you can produce now.

It's kind of frightening for a perfect kid who was Number One for what seems forever. It's a scene that can invite awareness that all he did was work and achieve to get ahead and stay ahead. And, now that he has achieved his goals, it seems to have all vanished. This awareness might raise the question, "Was it all worth it?" The rush to achieve is now replaced by silence. What do parents and their star students talk about now? Maybe college, careers, but that's the stuff for August not now in June. Silence is the order of the day!

The labor of the dazzle, hype, and promotion of their child is also over for the parents, and there's nothing to take its place. It's like being an agent for a star singer who suddenly decides to give up his career and retire. He no longer has need for an agent to promote him and make sure he stays well known and famous and has a unique, special style as an entertainer. For these parents, there is no one to promote anymore. Some friends suggest they volunteer to help the homeless.

It's not so easy to let go of the persona that these parents have cultivated. They were stars also and were a major part, maybe "the major part," of their child's school success. They opened doors for him, pushed him to achieve, and spent their afternoons, evenings, and weekends driving him to extra classes and activities that would build up his college application. They didn't take vacations or trips to the Caribbean or indulge in any fun time. They were dedicated to their child's success. And, they did it. So why now do they feel so empty, out of the running, and no longer a somebody like their son? Now they're just Mr. and Mrs. Morris; they're no longer known as Jerry Morris's parents. The curtain has closed on that life, and they are on stage with no next act in sight.

The parents of standard-bearers are also commodities that are valued by the school and community, but when that persona has disappeared, they no longer serve as "instruments of gain and objects of use." Without their star student basking in the limelight of success, they have now become Mr. and Mrs. who? And they somehow are unable to be thankful for the memories and go on. It's as if their main purpose in life, their reason for being, has left, leaving them to wonder how they can, if ever, replace the loss. Not so much the loss of their child moving on to college, but the loss of being a star like their child, of traveling in his or her limelight and circles, and of being a shaker and doer, a somebody.

Being a star student and a star parent is a sought-after role. However, it brings with it subtle costs that at first are hard to understand and, over time, to confront. In this role, both star students and parents are treated as special—"star" is the right word—who appear sure of themselves, their path, and their future. There is an aura about them that says, "They get it," and "They've got it all figured out." They seem worthy, entitled to their current and future success. They appear different—some would say they are "blessed"—from other kids and parents who are struggling to find their way.

But that aura and cloak of entitlement covers up an angst that comes with privilege for many star students. The story of this angst is often kept hidden and smoothed over by planning for the future, by a searching out of every angle of self-promotion that never ceases. Sometimes the use of drugs and alcohol is the only way to stop this quest and find some quiet.

The following chapters will explore the role of school administrators, guidance counselors, and teachers who appear to be solely interested in their star students' success and their own prestigious role as educators of star students. They too are trapped in a school world that values some students and parents more than others. Their consumer-driven school world uses educators as well as good news kids and parents as "instruments of gain." They are the teachers, counselors, and administrators of star students, and their careers are intertwined with their good news kids' success and status. They are the advanced placement course teachers, guidance counselors responsible for college admissions, and administrators who promote the success of the school.

They're all in it together. They are the elitists who teach, counsel, and lead elite students and who benefit from consumer-driven schooling. These are the teachers, counselors, and administrators the bad news kids of the school rarely encounter. Their teachers, counselors, and administrators are not members of the elite team nor are they seen as "instruments of gain and objects of use." They, like the bad news kids and their parents, exist and survive below the surface, under the radar. They are not star educators, kids, or parents. They inhabit a separate school world meant for the less worthy, a world occupied by kids who generate bad news for the school and community and by educators who rarely receive accolades for their work. They are the minor league players in consumer-driven schooling. They are seen as having not much to offer, as unworthy of any mention or distinction. They are not big leaguers.

The next chapter will examine the role of bad news kids and parents—bad news parents who are labeled by PTA leaders as "the parents who should be heard but who never show up."

NOTES

1. Alan Schwarz, "Risky Rise of the Good-Grade Pill," http://www.nytimes.com/2012/06/10/education/seeking-academic-edge-teenagers-abuse-stimulants.html?pagewanted=all (accessed June 11, 2012).

2. Alan Schwarz, "In Their Own Words: 'Study Drugs,'" www.nytimes.com/interactive/2012/06/10/education/stimulants-student-voices.html (accessed June 11, 2012).

3. Judith Warner, "Parents Created This Problem, and Must Address It," http://www.nytimes.com/roomfordebate/2012/06/09/fewer-prescriptions-for-adhd-less-drug-abuse/parents-have-fueled-the-abuse-of-adhd-medications (accessed June 10, 2012).

4. William L. Fibkins, "No Easy Way Out: Stories about American Adolescents," unpublished manuscript (2006), 59–62.

Chapter Three

The Cost to Bad News Kids and Parents

This chapter's focus is on the perception that many bad news kids and parents have of their high school. It's a negative perception that describes a consumer-driven school world in which they don't count. They are not objects that can be used for gain to market their school. They are present but have no positive role because they are viewed as having little to contribute except resistance and giving their school a bad name.

Bad news kids are different from good news kids. Usually when they arrive at high school they have a record of failure and acting out; they are persons of interest who are carefully watched. As a result, they get caught making mischief, get detentions, and are often suspended. Good news kids avoid the bad kid label by being smart enough not to get caught. They may do stimulant drugs, but they are not carefully watched or identified as persons of interest. Their acting out behavior is done undercover, so no one notices until the behavior gets out of control.

The light that shines on student behavior is much more intense for the bad news kids while the good news kids who act out are covered by the shadows of goodness. Not seen or ignored, the acting out of good news kids is not in the realm of possibility. As Alan Schwarz suggests in "In Their Own Words: 'Study Drugs,'" (see chapter 2), it's a story that just can't be true for star students. Our best and brightest don't act out, only the bad news kids.

They are the anti–good news kids. No advanced placement courses, SAT exams, college applications, college visits, college prep counseling, or honors at graduation (if there is one) for them. They may share the same hallways and lunch at McDonalds (different tables and conversations) with good news kids, but their destination after high school is more tenuous. Bad news kids and their parents know they are not going anywhere but the Army or the unemployment line.

So it comes as no surprise that bad news kids make the teachers, counselors, administrators, and parents of good news kids nervous. It's like having termites in a perfect home. The home looks good from the outside, but there are active pests bent on chewing away the beautiful facade and exposing it as a risky dwelling. That's what bad news kids do for and to their schools. They are a constant source of trouble that can destroy the image of a highly successful school that works hard to meet the needs of all its students. At least that's the description used by the school's media self-promotions and local real estate agents trying to lure newcomers to the community.

As a result, the bad news kids get little or no attention in the school's media output. That's the territory of good news kids and their parents, the doers and shakers whose actions and activities push a platform that says, "Hey, voters, you got an excellent school here. Look what the best and brightest of our students are accomplishing. And look how they are being given a top-notch education by our excellent teachers, counselors, and administrators. No wonder our college acceptance rate ranks among the best at the county and state level, and even at the national level."

The community image of the school is skewed toward the star students. Those are the students you read about in school newsletters and the local newspaper. You get a steady diet of good news that says all is well, news that says you can go back to sleep after you vote yes for the budget. Does this public-relations blitz censor out the bad news kids? The school and community grapevine is ripe with news about the bad news kids acting out. Newspaper police reports often cite cases of bad news kids being taken drunk from school to the hospital or of gang fights at school dances and sports events. But these deeds don't make the headlines.

Bad news kids understand their role in school organizations. They are usually given the poorest teachers and the easiest courses. The underlying message is, Behave, don't make waves, and all will be well. You'll graduate, but if you start trouble you'll be out of here. You don't have friends in high places like the good news students and parents. If you try to ruin the good reputation of our school, there will be consequences for your behavior.

Bad news kids are not "instruments of gain and objects of use" in consumer-driven schools. They know it. They know there is no way or place for them to make a contribution. It's not their school, and they soon sense they are not worthy of respect. So why try? They know they carry many labels: "those kids," "troublemakers," "druggies," "lazy," "good for nothings," "stragglers," "procrastinators."

It's as if they arrived in a supposedly democratic institution but they have no voting rights. The school world they inhabit is at the margins of school life. They are on the outside, looking into a world of seemingly happy good news kids enjoying high school life and planning a wonderful future. It's sort of like a Hollywood movie in which elegantly clad, well-to-do members of the community dance to beautiful music while the less fortunate bad news kids are outside with little chance of being welcomed to the dance.

And this outside-looking-in role is also shared by the parents of bad news kids. They avoid school as much as possible because it means trouble for them as well as their children. The bad news parents also carry many labels: "I've never seen her at the PTA workshops even though she needs it more than anyone"; "If you ask me, the apple doesn't fall far from the tree"; "She was a hell raiser like her kid and forced to drop out"; "She's got no time for the kids—always out partying."

The bad news parents are at the margins of school and community life. They're trying to fit in somewhere and be a part of something good, but the doors always seemed closed. What can they possibly contribute in a school based on a consumer-driven culture of getting ahead and staying ahead? There is nothing in this culture for them or their child, as their presence offers nothing of gain or use. They are viewed as an empty suit, as trouble, as not an asset to be cultivated and included.

For bad news parents, being summoned to school is a nightmare. No wonder many don't show up. First, there is the perfunctory meeting with the assistant principal for discipline who takes out the child's folder and recites all of his wrongdoings: "constantly speaks out in class," "does not finish class work or turn in homework," "makes fun of his business teacher," "skips class," "smokes in the bathroom," "makes fun of nice kids," and on and on. Then there is the meeting with all their child's teachers, who sit with their black lesson-plan books open and drone on and on about his lack of effort and bad behavior, saying in chorus that they're ready to "throw up their hands and give up."

And finally, there is the meeting with the school psychologist, who suggests,

Your son is in need of help, help we can't provide for him as our present counseling staff is overwhelmed with college admissions, testing, scheduling, and discipline counseling. Your son needs personal counseling. Here's the phone number for our local mental health clinic. I should warn you they too are overwhelmed so you may have a long wait before he is seen. Good luck and we hope he can make a fast turnaround or I'm afraid expulsion is in his future.

Thanks for coming by and I hope these meetings were helpful. By the way, the PTA has asked Dr. Fritz Lyons, director of the University Counseling Center, to speak at next Thursday's meeting at 7:00 p.m. in the library. His topic is "The Destructive Child." Can you make it? Oh, I'm sorry, you have to work. Well, do you have any questions? If not, it was nice meeting you.

Bad news parents usually stagger out of these no-good-news conferences. It should come as no surprise that they might be heard to mutter, "I could use a drink" on their way out.

Being a parent of a bad news kid is often a long, negative, haul. Difficulty with school often starts in the early grades and escalates as the student becomes known to teachers, counselors, and administrators as a problem. And, when kids have problems that disrupt the classroom, parents are brought in. In the court room, it is called "building a case," and by the time bad news kids get to high school, the folder that contains their transgressions may require a forklift to carry it. For the parents, it's a life of scaling down their hope and ambitions for their child until there is a gradual giving up on their part. They lose hope that things can turn around.

Many have tried to be good parents amid a series of devastating family problems. They had faith and hoped that one day their children would abandon their dark side and be like normal, successful kids. For many, that day never arrives. They are left guilty and confused, wondering what they did wrong. They never let themselves off the hook of blame. And every time the school calls, it's another dagger to their heart and hope. No one in the school wants to hear about how they tried and how difficult their child's life has been.

As one mother told me, "We've been written off. You can see it in the assistant principal's eyes. All they're interested in is finding a way to fast exit our kids." Meanwhile, the good news kids are envied by these parents. Everything seems right with them. These kids just seem so perfect compared to their own children. Why would they even think about going to a PTA meeting? They'd be a laughingstock, given their kid's bad reputation.

Parents who attend PTA meetings usually have children who do well in school. It's a club for the good news kids' parents, a club where good news parents have the opportunity to brag a little, or a lot, about their child's latest honors and achievements, as well as to listen to a child psychologist lecture about successful child-rearing, at which the PTA members feel they are the experts. Of course, the child psychologist laments the fact that those parents who really need this information are no-shows. He applauds the presence of the good news kids' parents by saying, "I feel I am speaking to the choir."

Bad news parents who feel like the unwashed often miss the point that they have much in common with the good news parents. Yes, on the surface all is well with the good news crowd. But beneath this cover-up there are cracks in the facade. There is the ongoing push to get ahead and stay ahead, the pressure to ace the next exam, SAT, advanced placement test, or college interview. No, they are not being summoned to school to be called on the carpet about their child's failures and behaviors. But they are constantly on call to make sure their star student gets one up on his or her peers. There is always the fear of failure, and good news parents often blame themselves when their seemingly perfect child falters.

So bad news and good news parents can have much in common. Many feel responsible, or on the hook for blame, when bad news visits their children. Hopes get dashed, and parents are suddenly abandoned by the perfect parent club. In the best of all worlds, wouldn't it be wonderful if the good news and bad news parents could share their loneliness and growing isolation when the bottom falls out of their child's life? And wouldn't it be wonderful if bad news and good news kids could share their broken world and find some common ground together? Bad news kids who have failed much of their lives might have some helpful advice for good news kids who fail for the first time, and vice versa. Failure can have many positive lessons.

Bad news parents should be careful what they ask for when they wish their family could be more like a good news family. It's often not the pretty picture with no problems that it seems to be. Good news parents should be careful not to belittle bad news parents because one day they too might have to deal with their child's poor behavior and/or failure. They might need a little advice from the failure pros.

In the best of all worlds, the good news kids who falter would be able to begin the process of shedding their role as an instrument of gain and would come to realize they are persons of dignity and respect. And bad news kids would come to realize that not being an instrument of gain has its advantages, helping them to realize they live in a world in which a little effort on their part might help to elevate their status and create a school world in which they too could achieve dignity and respect by getting off the failure train and beginning to take care of the business of school. It would be a school world in which the good news kids who are usually isolated in the skybox of privilege and the bad news kids who are often isolated on the bleachers of failure could share a common life.

As Michael Sandel suggests, democracy does not require perfect equality, but it does require that citizens share a common life. What matters is that people of different backgrounds and social positions encounter one another, and bump up against one another, in the course of everyday life. This is how we learn to negotiate and abide our differences, and how we come to care for the common good.[1]

The bright light that shines on bad news kids and parents often fails to reveal what their out-of-school life is like and the drama they experience day by day. Knowing more about their "story" might make their lives more understandable to us; it might make teachers, counselors, administrators, and even good news kids and parents more accepting and caring. The lives of bad news kids don't center on grades, exams, talk of college, and pushing for honors. Their lives center around surviving, trying to figure out how to dodge the emotional bullets being fired at them, and getting something right in a life that has had too many wrongs.

Here are some stories of why there is no easy way out for bad news kids and parents.[2] These stories may help educators better understand that while bad news kids and parents may not be objects of use and gain, they are entitled to the same kind of support and guidance as good news kids and parents.

I WAS ALWAYS TROUBLE SO THEY PASSED ME ALONG

Check my attendance. I usually miss more than forty days a year. Even in the first grade I would get sick on purpose so I wouldn't have to go to school. I hated it from the start. When I was in school I was MIA, missing in action. I had no idea what was going on. So what did I do? Like any other kid who is out of the loop, I acted out and raised hell. Even back then they tried to put me in resource rooms and special classes, but I wasn't having any of that.

My mother was on my side and she came to school and fought them every time. She wasn't having any of this crap of her kid being a resource room kid. I may not be a prep or a jock but I am not dumb. So they passed me along. They didn't want me coming back, and sure as hell they didn't want to deal with my mother when she got going. Sometimes I wonder if I would have liked school better if those early years had been different. But they weren't.

By the time I got to middle school I didn't know zip. Who wants to go to school when all the other kids know the stuff and you're in la-la land? And my mother gave up on fighting the school. And I guess she gave up on me amounting to anything. She got tired of it all. That's when I started smoking and drinking. We had our own little group that used to smoke out in the back of the school and in the bathrooms.

The other kids called us the "losers" of the school. But I think the preps and the jocks were sort of envious of us. They had to study and get ready for college. All we did was have fun, hang out, drink wine coolers and six-packs, smoke, and have sex. We were all like a family. We didn't do well in school, and if there was some trouble in town, we usually had something to do with it.

Our parents weren't the PTA type or those who went to open house. Our parents knew that if they set one foot in the school they would be accosted by teachers armed with complaints. You know, in PTA meetings they would talk about the "parents who should be here but aren't." They were talking about our parents. We were the outsiders, the misfits, the slackers, the smokers, the "losers," and we were proud of it. It was all we had.

It was true that our group was all we had. Most of us were poor. A lot of the kids' parents were divorced. Many of them worked two or three jobs to keep things going. Only a few people had medical coverage, so when you got sick or hurt, you made the most of it. We weren't the Little League type or those who went to summer camp or SAT camp. We weren't going to college and we knew it. Our parents didn't fit into the yacht club set. They were on the outside, like us. They were the adult "losers" of the town.

When I got to high school, things began to tighten up. They nailed you for everything: coming in late, smoking, cutting class, driving fast in the parking lot. According to the assistant principal, I had more detentions in one year than any former student. You might say I was setting records. The assistant principal spent more time with me than he did with his wife. I was smoking so much and so addicted that I couldn't stay in school for more than two classes. Then I would hang out with my friends or else take off. It was so stupid. Here I was so addicted to cigarettes that they kept busting me because

I had to go out and get a smoke. They didn't understand that I had no choice. Hell, the teachers had their own room to smoke.

Why were the kids getting busted for a habit they couldn't shake? So when they asked me to leave school and take the GED program, I wasn't surprised. That's what was happening to most of our gang. One by one we were knocking ourselves off or the school was doing it to us. I tried to hang on, thinking that if I waited them out they would pass me to get rid of me. But it didn't work. High school is different. You can't hide. But I wasn't going to any GED with all those morons. I tried joining the Army but they told me I needed a diploma or a GED.

So I'm home doing nothing. Maybe I'll go back to school next year or maybe I'll go to Florida or Kuwait to work in construction. I've seen the ads in the paper: "Big Salaries to Help Rebuild Florida and Kuwait." I'll come back and show these preps and jocks some day. What do I need their lousy diploma for?

THERE'S NO LIVING DOWN A BAD REPUTATION

I can hear the little wimps talking to each other when I come into class: "Smell the smoke on her, doesn't she know about taking care of herself?" Sure, I smoke, I drink, and I take some drugs. But what business is it of those little wimps to make fun of me or think they're so healthy? You see, I know what I'm doing. It's not like I'm an alcoholic or a drug addict. I like the taste of beer when I'm having a cigarette. As for grass, I don't do it a lot but it makes me feel really mellow.

It's not an everyday thing or something new. I've been smoking and drinking since the sixth grade. I get a kick out of these little nerds hitting on me because I hang out a lot. At least my friends and I don't go overboard the way these so-called model students do every weekend. It's such a joke! A lot of the nerds and jocks that put me down are the same ones who sign the sports pledge not to drink or take drugs while they're on a school team. But you ought to see them at parties on weekends.

They're drunk and stoned all over the place, falling down, driving a hundred miles an hour, and vandalizing people's lawns and mailboxes. Look at all the torn-up lawns and beer bottles all over the town on Sunday mornings. I can tell you it's not me or my friends who pull that stuff. If these jocks' mommies and daddies knew what their little babies were doing partying on weekends, they would die. And these are the same kids who belong to

SADD, Students Against Drunk Driving, and whose parents are always at those drug and alcohol workshops.

In some way, I feel sorry for some of these kids. It's like they're leading a double life. They sign this pledge because their parents and the school put pressure on them to do it. It's like the in thing to do, you know, having a drug-free school or town. That's a laugh. Did you ever see a drug-free school? Just look at all the parents who booze it up! Then their kids get thrown into the party world and they can't deal with the pressure. So they break the pledge and feel like liars. How would you feel if they put your picture in the town paper as one of the students who have signed a pledge not to drink or take drugs and to help keep your school drug free?

They shouldn't have this pledge stuff. It turns kids into liars. Let's face facts, kids are going to experiment. But these goody kids have to hide it and they go overboard. For what purpose? So we can have this big lie that our school and town are drug free? These kids don't seem to know any middle ground; like I said, they go overboard. I was at a party last week where this ninth grader drank fifteen, you got me, fifteen straight shots of vodka and no one stopped her. They were laughing at her stumbling around and taking her clothes off. She didn't have a clue to what was going on.

Finally, she started vomiting so bad that someone had to call the police. They took her to the hospital and had her stomach pumped. Hell, she could have died. Do you know what it's like for a young kid like that to come back to school on Monday with everyone talking about her? It's sheer terror! It's something she'll never live down. The do-gooders in the PTA will all be buzzing about it and people will knock her parents. No one ever thinks about the poor kid and what she's going through. What a price to pay for one night of craziness! The good thing is that maybe she'll learn her limits and watch out. Better now than later.

You've got to know who you are and what you're doing out there. Thank God I don't buy all of this clean-living stuff. The jocks and the nerds have it tough because they're expected "to be good," "to be smart," "to be good athletes," you know, "to lead the All American life." Believe me, no one expects that of me. I'm just going along and I'll make it. I'll get a good job or go to college. They say there is a college for everyone.

SHE WOULD NEVER MAKE IT TO THE JUNIOR PROM

I'll never make it to the junior prom. It's a sure thing. Bet on it. Hell, I wasn't even going to make it to my junior year. It's just something you know when you come from a family like mine. You see, none of us Gilmartinis ever amount to much. The school secretaries are always saying, "Oh, you're one of those Gilmartinis." That's the code for saying, "Oh, you're from that family. They never last here. You'll never amount to much."

I'm not on the list of ass-kissers that the teachers and secretaries fall all over. No matter what I do in school, good or bad, I'm forever "just one of those Gilmartinis." The kind of kid which the school never expects much from except trouble. No one in my family got their diploma; they all got thrown out or left for work. The big stretch limos never pulled up at our house to take my brothers or me to proms or parties. Hell, I have never even owned a dress. Maybe when I was a little kid I had one, but all I've worn from elementary school on is jeans and a jacket.

I always keep myself covered up. I don't know why. Maybe it's because I always have to share a room with one or more of my brothers. I've never had my own room. I've had no privacy, the only girl in a house with six boys. Plus I'm fat, obese really. I know for sure that's one reason why I always cover myself up. I'm ashamed of the way I look with all those rolls of fat. That's why the kids at school call me "She-man." I dress like a guy: layers of sweaters, jeans, and a jean jacket. I hear them calling me "gay girl" and "lesbian" behind my back. It hurts so much.

That's why I get in so many fights. I just explode when I hear kids calling me gay. What do they know? They don't even know me and they think they have the right to call me those things? They don't understand that I don't have any other clothes. My clothes are my brothers' hand-me-downs. No one ever buys me anything, not even at Christmas. Someday I would like to wear something feminine and soft and not look so tough.

I wonder what it must be like, growing up like a real girl and doing girl things. And what would it be like to be thin? I can't lose any weight at home! All my father wants me to do is cook pasta. I try to tell him about the nutrition stuff I've been learning in health class but he doesn't listen. My mother says all he wants is his pasta. If I never see another tortellini again, I'll be ecstatic! If the other kids had to do all the cooking and eat what I eat, they'd be fat like me.

My business teacher says I have beautiful eyes and would look great if I lost weight. I've tried but it doesn't work. I know she likes me, but even she doesn't understand how hard it is for me in my family. No one does. I can't help the way I look. I don't have a choice. You see, I'm a slave at home. My mother always says, "It's the girl's job to clean, cook, and do the laundry." She's from what she calls "the old country," Italy. She was raised to wait on her father's and brothers' every desire. She was a slave and now she expects the same from me.

She works a double shift at the state hospital so I never see her. She just leaves me a list of what to do and I've got to do it. If I don't, my father will give me "the belt." If dinner is not ready and the house cleaned by the time he gets home from work, he won't hesitate to whip me. He'll say, "Get in my room." He makes me take down my panties and hits me with the belt on my buttocks. Sometimes he hits me so hard that I have big open sores where the buckle hits me.

That's why I never dress for gym. I'm afraid the teacher or the other kids will see the blood or the marks. It's easier to cut the class and take a failure. I'm never going to graduate so what's the difference? I don't want the school finding out and calling my father. He'd really beat me if that happened. It's always been the same way, since I was a kid. My brothers never have to lift a finger. I have to make their beds, wash their clothes, do their ironing, make dinner, do the dishes, and take out the garbage. If things aren't right, dishes not done right or if the soup is cold, I'm the one who gets the belt.

My father never hits my brothers. Once in a while my mother will stick up for me but my father tells her to shut up or she'll get the belt too. I know he's hit her before. I think that's why she works a double shift; she doesn't want to be home. She just leaves me to deal with it. I used to think, "Some mother, leaving me to do all this shit." But she can't change things. I guess she's just trying to save herself. And I never get an allowance for all this work. I'm probably the only kid at school who didn't order a class ring.

My one hope is that someday I'm going to get out of here. I have to be eighteen before I can sign myself out. I could drop out now but my father would have to okay that. He did it for my brothers. But he would never do it for me. He needs his slave! At school they think I'm "just another Gilmartini" and that I don't care. They don't understand that I need to get out of my house before I can even start to live. I guess other kids will look back at their high school years and talk about the junior prom and the limos. I know I'll look back and feel bad for myself.

Now I just want to get out and forget about my life as a teenager. I can hardly wait until the day my father and my brothers have to cook their own pasta and clean. Maybe then they'll appreciate and love me.

NO PLACE LIKE HOME

I'm living downstairs in the basement with my boyfriend. My older brother is living upstairs with his girlfriend and her little kid, and my other brother is living out in the back room with his girlfriend and her kid. And guess what? My grandparents are coming up from Florida to spend the winter with us. Great life, right! And what are my parents doing about it? Squat, that's what. You'd think they would get fed up with all these kids. For Christ's sake, my brothers are in their twenties and they still don't have a job or a place to live. And my parents put up with it. They should throw the bums out, but do they? No!

My parents are never home. They both work two jobs. What a marriage! Even my boyfriend is a loser. He's another one who has no job or place to live. He doesn't even have a GED from high school. How I landed up with this creep is beyond me, but I don't have the heart to throw him out. I mean, I'm just a kid, a high school junior, and I've got all this crap floating around me. It's like a zoo. I can't study or concentrate on anything with these little kids screaming and carrying on. Hell, they're not even members of my family.

My brothers are suckers just like me. We were always bringing home stray dogs and cats. But now it's stray people. And this whole thing with the school makes me laugh. Whenever I miss a day or cut out, they call home but they never can get my parents. My parents don't want to be bothered with that BS. Then they call me in and tell me I better shape up. Hell, they don't have any idea about my life or what goes on in my house. They'd crap if they did.

I look at all these nerd kids with their Mercedes and designer clothes and I laugh. Their life, with their moms making them breakfast and taking them shopping to Macy's, is so phony. Those kids would fold if they had half the problems I had. You see I had to be tough even when I was in the middle school. I was the one who was always blamed and sent to the office. There was something about me that always made me stick up for the underdog. I was forever getting into fights that had nothing to do with me so I could help some kid who was being bullied.

It goes back to taking in those stray dogs and cats. I never wanted to see anyone hurt. I was the only one in my class in elementary school that used to give gifts to all the kids who seemed poor. I still can't stand the idea of a kid going without a present for Christmas. That's why I want to become an elementary school teacher. I want to help all those kids who have troubles at home that no one knows about. You see, I can tell. I just look at a kid who has trouble and I know. It's like a magic power I have. I know I would have trouble with those pushy parents of smart kids, but maybe I could help them to not put so much pressure on them to be perfect, to be too good.

Maybe there's something good about my parents; at least they taught us not to turn our backs on people. Sometimes it's hard because you can't deal with all the pain in the world, even here in this small town. You think I'm happy every time I see an animal or person in trouble and I can't stop to help out? Well, I'm not. I wish sometimes that I could just drive by and ignore what's happening, look the other way. I think if that were true my life would be a lot easier and so would my brothers' and parents'.

We're all the same way. But I don't want to end up like my brothers: they're too good. They're both suckers for any hard luck story and look where it got them. My teachers tell me I have a gift to help people but I'm not much good at helping myself. They're right, but if they really knew my family, they would see why. How do I go from being my parents' daughter to someone who takes care of herself and helps other people?

I'LL START DOING MY SCHOOL WORK WHEN SHE STOPS BUGGING ME

It was always the same story every year. I never had a choice in anything to do with my school. My mother would worm her way in to pick out my teachers and scope out the best classes for me. And then she would bug me about what homework was due, the reports, and all the other assignments. It was endless. And, about November 1, I would do the same thing I had done every year before: I would stop doing the work.

I would tell her that I wasn't going to do anything until she stopped bugging me about school. It was that simple! But it never worked. Once the first report card came out, with comments like "Mark is almost always unprepared with this assignments," "Mark appears lethargic and uninterested," and "Mark might do better being in a lower-track class," she was up to school for a conference within twenty-four hours. And the outcome was always the same. I could predict the outcome word for word before she came back from the school. It was like a little game I would play with myself. I knew she would come in and yell up to me, "Get down to the kitchen right away."

We would sit at the kitchen table. That was the war room. And she would start in. "I'm up to here (pointing to her throat) with your lack of respect for me and yourself. I'm sick of going down to the school and being humiliated (then why was she going?). It's the same old story: homework and reports not in, poor test grades, cutting classes, appearing half dead to the teachers, and on and on. The only good thing they say about you is that you're a perfect gentleman and never cause any trouble. And I'm sick of hearing the same story, that you're a classic underachiever."

She hated hearing that because the therapist she took me to in the ninth grade told my mom that she was the problem and that I would never change until she left my school work to me. Needless to say, she pulled me out of therapy the next week.

"How are you ever going to survive in the real world? You're a junior already. What college is going to take a student with a C average? You are going to end up in some community college or the Army, if they'll take you. I don't know. Maybe the therapist was right. It's a lost cause. And to think your IQ is 140. Other kids would give their soul to have your gifts and all you can do is watch TV and eat. Your father and I have worked and saved all our lives to send you to a good college and for what?

"I'm done. I don't care what happens to your school work. You can graduate at the bottom of your class for all I care. Just remember one thing: You did it to yourself, young man. You can't blame your father or me. From now on it's your life. Don't mention any of this to your father when he comes home. I don't want to burden him with this after he's worked all day. I've got to make dinner. I suggest you go to your room and do some serious thinking about what you want to do with your life."

Wow! I'd think. Maybe I've done it. Maybe I've finally done poorly enough to get her to get off my case. Maybe I've won. Wouldn't it have been great to have had her off my back, not to have had to deal with all of that school stuff every day when I came home? Maybe we could have had a real conversation at the dinner table instead of the standard questions: "How did it go in school?" and "What's for homework tonight?" Maybe we could have stopped talking about college and who was applying to what school. I hated hearing about all my mother's friends whose kids were getting into Princeton and Dartmouth.

I wanted to get to know more about my mother but I couldn't because it was always school, school, and more school. My dad tried to help out. He would see that her approach was not working with me. But she was too much for him. She was the boss. After a while he would just shut up. My mother always said she was doing what she called this "loving nagging" because she didn't have anyone to help her when she was a kid. She always said she had wanted to go to college but she had no help.

I knew I was a big disappointment to her. I wasn't the child she wanted. She never said it, but I knew. But she wasn't the mother I wanted either—the odd couple for sure. I was leaving home next year, college or no college, and I didn't want to leave home with things like they were. But I didn't think things were going to change. I knew my mother. Come Tuesday, she'd be back at her cause, her life's work, nagging me. It always worked that way.

I just hope I never do the same thing with my kids. Mom and I were both trapped in a life about school and neither one of us would give in. I couldn't and she wouldn't. Or is it that I wouldn't and she couldn't?

MY FATHER LEFT HOME WHEN I WAS BORN

The early beginnings were a sign of things to come. I have never known my father and I hope I never see him. I'm afraid of what I might do to him for all he did to me. He left, so my mother says, when I was born. It was the first of many blows to come my way in life. I hate my father without having ever set eyes on the man. How can that be? After I was born, we moved in with my mother's father and her brother.

My grandfather was a wonderful man, like a father to me. My Uncle Frank was a bully who bossed and physically pushed everyone around. I guess you would call him an abuser today. If we were watching TV and he didn't like the show, he would change the channel without asking anyone. If anyone one of us said anything he would say, "Shut the hell up or I'll give you something to complain about." Even then I vowed that I would get even with him for bullying us; he would get what was coming to him.

When I went to school it was really strange. I found myself hating the other kids who had real parents, nice clothes, and lunch boxes. I felt different, especially when we had to fill out those forms asking for your parents' address, birthday, place of work, and so on. When it came to my father, I forced myself to write, "Unknown." Sometimes I wanted to lie, to put down my father as a doctor or lawyer, but I couldn't do it. I knew the teacher knew because the mail sent home from the school was always addressed to "Mrs." And not "Mr. and Mrs."

That's why I hated the other kids. They could fill out those forms and show they were from a normal family. I was sure there wasn't another kid whose father had left! I tried to get rid of this hate, it bothered me so, but I couldn't. And the worst part was that it showed. I couldn't hide it. All through elementary school and middle school, teachers would tell me to "lighten up" and "hang out," but it wasn't something I knew how to do.

I knew the teachers were right, but I felt like I was in a box and couldn't get out. Even my poor mother and grandfather noticed it and tried to get me involved with Boy Scouts, church, and Little League. But I hated it all. I was a lousy athlete and hated going to the games by myself while the other kids had their dads and family. My mother and grandfather were always working, and I certainly didn't want Frank there. I tried to make friends but the other kids stayed away from me. They thought I was weird and maybe I was.

I couldn't fit in. But when they started calling me "gay" and "homo" in middle school, it was more than I could take. Why did they say those things, those awful things? Hadn't I had enough? I didn't think I was gay, but what did it matter when everyone else said I was? In the eighth grade I missed a lot of school. I just couldn't, wouldn't go and take that name-calling day after day. I was bullied at home and now at school too.

Then my grandfather died. It was just before my graduation from eighth grade. It was the worst time in my life, again. He was the only person besides my mother who loved me. At the funeral some of the kids from school and their parents came. It was the first time anyone had ever been nice to me or showed they cared. It helped, but I was too busy worrying what was going to happen with the house. It didn't take long to find out.

My grandfather hadn't been dead a week when Frank told my mother that he had sold the house and we would have to move. My mother was a wreck. Where would we live? What if we had to move to another school district? She relaxed more when I told her I wanted out. I needed to move and make a fresh start. So we got a cheap apartment. Now it's really good. We don't have Frank to deal with and nobody in the new school knows anything about me and they don't seem to care. It's high school and no one cares whether your father is dead or alive. No one calls me "gay" or "homo" anymore.

All you have to do is show up, keep your mouth shut, and do your work. I can do that. Besides, I have a part-time job now and a car and I can go anywhere. In some ways my grandfather saved me, again. When he died, it allowed my mom and I to move on. He gave us the gift of a fresh start. I don't feel so boxed in anymore.

I'M HOMELESS AND MY PARENTS THINK I'M OKAY

I got off to a bad start in high school. My parents made me take French even though I barely passed it in junior high school. Plus they made me take sequential math and biology, things I hated. And I had the stupid orchestra that took one period each day. I had no lunch and no time to see my friends. I couldn't fit the art courses I really wanted to take into my schedule. My parents said I could take those courses once I got through with the college requirements. They were both teachers and they said that they knew what was best.

When we had my program appointment with the eighth-grade counselor, I kept telling them that I wouldn't be able to handle all that stuff. They just sat there and said, "You're an underachiever, but once you get to high school and the real world, you'll be able to do it. We know you will." They didn't like the junior high; they said that the school was "all fun and games" and that "learning wasn't taken seriously there." I had no chance to take what I wanted. The summer before high school I did my best to put it all out of my mind. Maybe my parents were right. Maybe I would do fine.

In September, things went along okay. But by October I hadn't a clue what was going on in math, science, and French. My first report card was horrendous, three Fs, two Ds, and a C in orchestra. I told my parents that I couldn't do it. I cried and did everything I could to get them to understand, but all they could say was "You have to do it. Take notes, go for extra help. We'll even get you a tutor. But you have to stick it out."

So they got me a tutor for math, science, and French. Now I had no time. I had to give up soccer for the stupid tutors. And on top of that, they grounded me on weekends "so you can make sure you do all you can do to get through these courses." I found myself not going home after school. What was the point? All that was waiting for me was a tutor and more talk about how school was going. So I lied. I told my parents I was staying for extra help or going to the library to study.

In reality, I just walked the school corridors by myself or sat out on the football bleachers. I used to think that this must be what it's like to be homeless, just wandering around. Once in a while a teacher would stop me on their way home and ask if everything was all right. I always told them I was getting the late bus home. Even the 5 o'clock bus driver said, "You must be a great student, staying after school and studying every day. Your parents must be proud of you."

I laughed to myself; if only he knew the real story. When too many people took notice of me, I would walk all the way home, even in the rain and snow. It was better than being home. I had created my only little world between three and six o'clock. It was my time! My parents couldn't find me and I could do what I wanted, more or less. Each day I would figure out something to do. I had my places. Some days I would go to the exercise trail in back of the high school and just walk. Other days I would sit by the bus stop and watch the kids that took the late bus home. The kids would look at me kind of funny but I didn't care.

Sometimes I would walk up to the deli and get a Coke and chips. That would take thirty minutes each way. I was always after some destination that would take time. Meanwhile, my parents seemed happy; they were proud of their "little girl who was finally taking her academics seriously." I had to laugh; I was homeless and they were happy. If only they knew the real story. They had their own little world and I had mine.

By December I was hopelessly behind. All my teachers were suggesting that I drop to a lower track. But I didn't care. Report cards weren't due until January. I laughed to myself that I still had a whole month to be "homeless." But then it all ended. I got a call to report to the assistant principal's office. He said that he had gotten a lot of reports that I had been seen around the building long after the other kids had gone home.

He said that he had checked the sports programs and the library and found I did not belong to a sports team or a study group. He sat back in his chair and asked, "Why are you hanging around after school every day? Don't you have a home to go to? What do your parents think about this? I checked your records and you're failing every course. Please tell me what's going on. I'll try to help you."

I burst into tears and told him how my parents wouldn't let me take the art courses and how I couldn't pass the math, science, and French no matter what I did. I told him that I hated going home and all I did each day was wander around until the five o'clock late bus. He laughed when I said I felt like I was homeless, but he stopped when he saw how serious I was. Finally he said, "I know you don't want me to do this but I have to call your parents and get them in here tomorrow. I promise that I won't tell them about what you have been doing after school unless they ask me a direct question. This can't go on. You'll get sick or break down. I promise I'll do what I can to change their minds about the courses."

When I got home my mom said that the assistant principal had called and wanted to see both her and my dad first thing the next day. She said, "What's this all about? What do you mean, you don't know? This never ends with you, does it? It's been one thing after another since you got to high school. Now we have to take a day off and deal with this. Your father will love this when he comes home. And just when we thought you were beginning to take some responsibility."

At the meeting the next day the assistant principal started off by telling my parents that he felt that the program I was enrolled in was too difficult for me. He told them that all this pressure for college courses wasn't worth the anguish that they were putting me through. "Besides," he said, "this must be making you miserable as well. Your daughter has no self-esteem or satisfaction in her work. You can't feel good about that. Is all this worth seeing your daughter so unhappy?"

As soon as he said that, I could see the look on my parents' faces. They had heard enough. They didn't like school administrators or counselors; my mom always said, "All they do is sit around their offices and mess with people's lives." And they didn't like anyone suggesting that their daughter take the "easy way out." This wasn't going to work.

Then I started to cry. It just happened. I looked at my parents and said, "Dad, Mom, look at things. I'm dumb. Well, maybe not dumb, but I can't pass these courses. I've tried to tell you in every way I could think of but you can't hear me. I've been tutored for extra help, I've given up my social and sports life, and I am failing and miserable. What do you want from me? Do you want to kill me? I'm over my head; even the teachers are telling me to quit. Why can't you listen?" I was crying so hard that the secretaries and kids in the office could hear me, but I didn't care. This wasn't fair.

I looked at my parents and said, "I'm not doing this anymore. I'm dropping math, science, and French, and orchestra too; I hate playing that stupid flute and I'm no good at it. I'm going to take some art courses next semester. I don't care if I don't graduate in four years. I'm going to major in art and go to art school after graduation. That's what I'm good at, not French, math, and science. That's not me and you can't force me back into those courses. Call the police, call the courts, tell the principal. I don't care. I'm not doing it anymore. I'm over my head and I'm sinking. I'm not doing it."

My parents just sat there. They couldn't believe I was saying these things and neither could I. Finally my mom said, "Well, this is not the time or the place for this. We'll talk about this tonight as a family. You've done quite enough to embarrass us." I looked at my mom and said, "We are not talking about this later. We are talking about this now! You understand me? Now! You think I'm embarrassing you now? You haven't heard anything yet. You think I've been staying after school every day to study?

"Well, that's a lie, a lie. I've stayed after because I don't want to go home. I'm homeless, you hear me? Homeless! All I do is wander around the school or the sports field until the last bus. I'm like a freak; all the other kids look at me like I'm a bag lady or something, but it's better than going home to tutors or your whining about my grades. That's the real reason you're here today: because the assistant principal has gotten reports about me hanging around. It's so sad that it's funny.

"You don't even know or care what's going on in my life. It's all your idea of grades and college. Don't you want me to be happy? Don't you want me to come home every afternoon and be happy and not have to hide out like I've been doing? Well, I don't care anymore what you think. I'm dropping math, science, French, and orchestra—that's it!"

I had them. There was nothing they could do. I had won. I couldn't believe it. I felt like a swimmer who had escaped the undertow, lying on the beach exhausted. My father said, "Well, it's your life. Maybe it is better that you change. All this conflict isn't worth it for some stupid college acceptance. I can't take much more either." He looked at the assistant principal and asked, "Where do we sign to allow these changes to happen?" And so I changed and took my art courses. I loved the courses and did well. A lot of the conflict in our family ended with that meeting. My parents never again tried to pick my courses.

Sometimes I wonder what would have happened to me if I hadn't fought back. Why did I have to become so crazy for them to understand? If I had been a good little girl and gone along, I would have drowned. Maybe I really would have become homeless. It's not good, ever, to go along with anyone or anything just because "they" think it's good for you, even your parents. Sometimes things have to get crazy before they get better.

THE BAD PARENT

I sometimes think to myself, what's better? To have good parents who are always doing everything for their kids in public, but when they get home they are mean and abusive to the kids? No one ever knows but the kids themselves, and who can they tell? No one would believe them. Or is it better to have parents like mine who are bad parents—at least to me. They don't mince any words. They like my sister better than me. We're both adopted but I'm the kid they don't want.

Don't get me wrong, they don't beat me up with a bat or anything like that. They just beat me up with words. Let me give you an example. If I need a ride to or from school, they will never do it. Even if I'm sick in school, my mother won't come and pick me up. The high school nurse knows better than to call her. She always says, "I shouldn't be telling you this but I feel so sorry for you. Is your mother always so unpleasant? I hate calling her on the phone. I can feel the hostility. I know you're adopted, but she has no right treating you like that. Here you are, running a fever, and I can't send you home.

"I really should call Child Protective Services, but what are they going to do? They're already over their heads with real abuse cases. They'll just make a house visit and things will probably end up being worse for you. How come she doesn't treat your sister that way? If I call about your sister, your mother or your dad is here within minutes. Does your mother know how abusive she is being to you?"

I think a lot about what the school nurse said, about Child Protective Services already being "over their heads with real abuse cases." Isn't my situation abusive? It feels like that to me. Sure, I live in a nice home, have my own room, plenty of food, decent clothes, but that isn't enough. I feel like my parents are watching my every move. Every time I take the car, they ask where I'm going and they check the mileage when I get home. I'm not allowed to have anyone else, particularly a girl, in my car. My father always checks the car to see that it isn't scratched. Most of the time I just ride my bike because it isn't worth the hassle.

I'm the only junior in the high school who still has a bike. It seems to me that every time I want to do something, the answer is "No." When my sister and I came to high school, I was the one who had to take industrial technology courses because my parents said that they couldn't afford two college tuitions at the same time. So my sister gets to take the academic classes while I get stuck with all the losers in the blow-off curriculum—"losers heaven," they call it. I had just as good grades as my sister in junior high, so why was I shoved off with the rejects? I hate saying that but it's true. None of the kids in my program want to be there. They want out of school. Each day is the same.

The kids fool around and try to get the teachers to throw them out. Besides, I hate all the technology stuff. Who needs auto mechanics, carpentry, electricity, and mechanical drawing? I taught myself all the stuff on my own. Why should I be going to school to learn things I know already? And the other courses are garbage; the Introduction to the Business World class is taught by a guy who has been there forever. They just keep moving him around, from program to program, hoping he drops dead. All he does is read from the book and ask us to take notes. It's all in the book so why should we be taking notes?

Half the time he falls asleep and the kids sneak out the door. Or the kids will ask for a pass at the beginning of the period and never come back. He never asks them where they were. He doesn't care; he just pretends not to notice. And the math class I'm taking is so easy. It's called Math in the Business World. It's all about learning how to keep a checkbook and do a budget. I've had a job on my own since seventh grade; I know all about that stuff.

And why am I taking this blow-off course when I passed three state exams in junior high in math with a 95 and got an A for the course? I was recommended for all academic courses with honors in math and science and where am I? In the bottom track! I keep telling my parents that I don't belong in these courses, but they say I have to learn something that I can use to make a living when I get out of school. Again, the same old line, "We can't afford two college tuitions. We'll be on a fixed income by then. Remember, we were older when we adopted you and your sister. We've tried to give you a good home, but we can't be expected to do everything. We just feel you're better suited to the work world, that's all.

"There will be no more discussion. You're never grateful for all we've done for you. Where would you be if we had not come along? In some foster home or back with your real mother? You should be down on your knees thanking God for finding you a good Christian home with us. Never satisfied, that's you, mister. The reason we're letting your sister go to college is that she's a girl; she'd never be able to leave high school and find a trade like you can. Besides, you can always go to college on your own if it's that important to you. What's the big deal about college anyway? Neither of us went, and we did okay."

It's always the same conversation, almost word for word. Why do I continue to ask? It hurts my ears. It's like hearing a tape on the wrong speed and not being able to turn it off. My mom and dad both have the same party line: fixed income, good Christian home, they made it without college, boys can make it without an education but girls can't. I'm in the wrong place at the wrong time. I'm not the kid they wanted, and they surely are not the parents I wanted. I don't fit. I think about what they say: "You should be down on your knees thanking God for finding you a good Christian home."

Maybe I should, but all I think about is being with my real mother. I always have this dream in which she comes to the door and tells my parents that she is taking me back. She is tall and beautiful, with a good education, and a big job. She takes me home and lets me take all the college prep courses. After high school, I get a scholarship to Princeton. But that day never comes. Sometimes when I hear a knock at the door or an unfamiliar voice on the phone, I actually think that she has come for me.

Where is she? Why has she abandoned me to these people, Mr. and Mrs. "No"? Maybe she had to. Maybe she couldn't support me and felt that I would have a better chance being adopted. Sometimes I even talk to her, telling her how unhappy I am and asking her to please come and take me "home." Once in a while, when I get up enough guts, I ask my adopted mother who my real mother was. But she always avoids the question, saying she doesn't know and to stop asking her.

But I know she knows something. There must be papers somewhere. When I get to be twenty-one, I'm going to find out. A part of me, though, is afraid to find out who she really is. What if she's in jail or a prostitute? What if she is not nice and is worse than my adopted parents? But I know she's not; I know she's a good parent and a good person. She would have come for me if she only knew how unhappy I am. I know she thinks I'm being well taken care of. She'd be here in a minute if she only knew. She's a good parent. She'd pick me up at school if I was sick. She's a good parent. I know.

COMING BACK FROM REHAB

Coming back from rehab wasn't easy. I could see the way some of the kids and teachers looked at me, like I was damaged goods or had the plague or AIDS. But you know what the toughest thing was? Not being able to smoke when I wanted and hang out with the friends I made in rehab. My new friends were like my family. We had been through a lot together and told each other things that no one else knew about. I could trust them with anything. In thirty days I had learned to open up and ask for help, something I never did in my whole life! I came to accept that I was an alcoholic, just like my father.

I had spent my whole life trying to help him and my friends while I just let myself go to hell. At first, I didn't buy the bullshit the therapist was saying. I didn't believe I was an alcoholic, and going to the hospital wasn't my choice. The court had given me a choice: going to rehab or going upstate to a detention home. Some choice! My friends gave me a big going-away party. That's the last time I had a drink. They all cried and told me they would come and visit and write. One of my friends had been in the same hospital, and he said it wasn't so bad. It was easy for him to say; he was out.

But the day I left home I was scared, shaking all over. On the way there my mother kept saying it was the best thing, that I would come out with a new outlook on life. She had become pretty discouraged about my drinking and smoking pot. I had started stealing money from her and even sold my stereo to get money for booze. I was even renting out my car at school to other kids who didn't have licenses to pick up a few bucks. I guess she finally had it when I used her bank card to withdraw a thousand dollars. I didn't even think about it. I just did it and blew the money partying and treating my friends.

When she called the police and brought charges against me, I couldn't believe it. But I knew I was out of control. I was doing crap in school and I looked like hell all the time. I couldn't sleep or go to school without a drink. It's amazing how long you can go on drinking and drugging yourself to death without anyone noticing. The school just thought I didn't care. I would come in late every day and then leave early. I had a million detentions. They tried suspending me and threatening summer school, but what could they really do? After a while you wear them down and they give up on you.

I learned at the hospital that alcoholics are like that: they know just what buttons to push to keep people off their backs. The main job is keeping the booze and drugs coming! It's that simple and that complicated. People can't help you when you don't want their help. On the way to the hospital, I looked at my mother and noticed how old she had become. She had been through all the alcoholic craziness with my father until she finally left him. And now, I was putting her through the same crap.

It felt so strange. I used to hate to see my father drinking. Once he picked up the first drink I knew he would start yelling at my mother and hanging out with his friends at the bars. He had four DWIs before they forced him into rehab the first time. After that he was in and out of rehab but nothing worked. He always went back to the booze and his crazy friends.

Now he was living with some woman who was into crack. My mother never talked about him. She always said it took too much out of her to think or worry about him. It had taken her years of therapy to get to the point where she could go on with her life. And now she was going through it with me. I had become out of control just like my father. How had I let that happen when I had seen what the booze did to him and our family? At the hospital I would learn that I didn't have any control once I picked up "the first drink," just like my dad.

For the first time I was aware, and it scared me, that I was like him. I just hoped that I would get better, that the rehab would take, and that I wouldn't relapse like my father. Maybe my mother would be able to get some rest while I was in the hospital. When we drove into the hospital grounds, I felt like hell physically and emotionally. I was scared but I knew I couldn't go on like I was. I wanted to get better.

The first few days at the hospital were a nightmare. I was in this section with about twenty other high school kids. They told us we couldn't make phone calls or have calls come in for the first week, and after that only if we went to all therapy and recreation meetings. It was like a jail, and the other kids looked like some of the kids I had only seen on TV: wild hair and grubby looking. A lot of them had been on crack and cocaine and were having a tough time detoxing. I could hear them hallucinating at night, screaming, and banging the walls with their heads.

I was so scared! And there was no getting away from it. My roommate was in for alcohol and cocaine addictions. She was also anorexic. She looked like hell: big black bags under her eyes and shaking all over. However, after a week things started to get better. The tranquilizers began to work and people started to open up in the therapy group. Some of the stories of physical and sexual abuse were horrible.

One girl had been raped repeatedly by her stepfather for ten years! No wonder we had all turned to the booze and drugs; the stuff worked to relieve the pain. For me, I learned that I started the booze both to get relief from all the pain my father brought me and my mother, and, in some crazy way, to get closer to my father. The therapist said I couldn't get close to him in any way so I decided to be like him, to join him, to become the girl with the glass in her hand just like my dad was the guy with the glass in his hand.

I told the group how I couldn't stop calling my father and going to visit even though he was always drunk. I knew it was bad for me, I could feel it, but I just needed to be with him or hear his voice. I wanted him to love me. Somehow I thought if I kept in touch with him, he would get better. But he never did. In fact, just the opposite happened. I started to drink with him. It was like our communion. It was the only thing that we had in common, that we could share: the bottle. It was the only time I wasn't uneasy or afraid of him.

The therapist said I was lucky that I was getting help before I ended up like my father. She said I had to learn to separate myself from my father. She cautioned that this would be hard and my father would not let go easily. Alcoholics don't give up; they know how to push your buttons. I know; I was one of them.

I left the hospital after thirty days; they wanted me to stay longer but I felt I could handle things. The plan was that I would come back for therapy once a week and go to AA meetings every few days. My mother picked me up. I could tell that she was scared; I was too. A lot had happened in thirty days. For the first time in years I was calm and I looked great. I had always thought I was ugly, but the group had taught me that I was attractive and smart.

On the way home, my mother did most of the talking. She said that my father and my friends had called and asked if they could stop by when I got home. She had told them that it was up to me. It was happening just like the therapist said it would. I wasn't out of the hospital five minutes and I had to start making decisions that could hurt or help me. Like my group said, it's so much easier being high because you don't have to deal with anything. Being sober is harder. You feel things you don't want to: anxiety, threats, joy, disappointment, pain.

I knew I wanted to see my friends, but I didn't want to get back into their lifestyle. I needed to meet people who were straight, and I hoped I would do that at AA. And I wanted to see my father but I wasn't ready for that yet. I just wanted to go home and have a good dinner with my mom. I wanted to tell her how much I loved her and admired the way she led her life. She was the one who had saved me and helped me to save myself.

Then I wanted to go to an AA meeting. There was one at our church at seven o'clock. I was uneasy about that. I knew I would see people from the neighborhood or even some teachers from school. The therapist had told me I would feel that way but that "alcoholism affects many families . . . you'll be surprised who you'll find at the meetings."

So we went home and kept it simple. We had my favorite dinner, lasagna, and hugged and cried a lot. My mother said she knew she would be on edge for a while, particularly if my old friends and my father came back into my life. But she realized that she couldn't start watching me. My recovery was up to me. I was so glad she said that because I didn't know how I was going to handle a lot of things.

It was all new. I had to take one day at a time. At seven I drove to the church. I knew I had to be there but I was very nervous walking in. There were a lot of people standing around drinking coffee and smoking. Most of them seemed older. Just as I was pouring myself a cup of coffee, someone gave me a pat on the back and said, "Hi, my name is Jerry and I'm an alcoholic."

I turned around and it was my father. He gave me a big hug and said he had been sober for thirty days, ever since I went into rehab, and that my going for help somehow had given him the courage to start going to meetings again. He had moved out of his old house and gotten a new apartment. He even had a job! I couldn't believe it. Then he said he had to go, he was making a presentation that night.

He wrote down his address and phone number and said, "Give me a call when you're ready. You have a lot on your plate right now. I didn't plan on seeing you here tonight. It's probably too much for both of us. Take some time for yourself and call me when you're ready. I hurt you and your mom a lot and I'm trying somehow to make amends for it all, but we can't do that in one night. I love you."

And then he was gone, up to the podium. It a few minutes he stood up and said, "My name is Jerry, and I'm an alcoholic. I've been sober for thirty days. They asked me to talk tonight about asking forgiveness from the people I've hurt." He talked for twenty minutes about how he had hurt my mother, me, and himself. I cried the whole time. After the meeting he waved good-by to me from across the room and said, "See you soon." He never mentioned to anyone that his daughter was there.

On the way home I thought about what a day it had been. When I got home I didn't tell my mother about the meeting. Keep it simple, right? She was still dealing with me. I didn't want to complicate her life. For the first time since I was a kid, we were all happy, me, my mother, and my father, separate but happy—a strange thing. And I wasn't hoping, like I used to do, that my parents would get back together again. I was just happy to be at peace. I had to get to bed so I would be ready for school in the morning.

I laughed at myself. Some kids had got awards for being the first to get As or run a thousand yards. Me, I was the first student in the high school to come back from rehab. I laughed again; at least I was first in something. I wondered if they would run my story in the school newspaper. Would they title it "Miss Rehab Returns to Scene of Former Drug and Alcohol Abuse"?

My life is sure a story!

NOTES

1. Michael J. Sandel, *What Money Can't Buy: The Moral Limits on Money* (New York: Farrar, Straus and Giroux, 2012).

2. William L. Fibkins, "No Easy Way Out: Stories about American Adolescents," unpublished manuscript (2006), 23–24, 31–37, 48–50, 63–69, 80–85, 125–26, 137–41.

Chapter Four

The Cost to High School Principals

The role of a high school principal involves much more than education. The role requires them to be skilled politicians, always on the lookout for positive votes, nurturing a cadre of followers, students, parents, and community members whom they can employ to support their efforts.

In return, these students, parents, and community members are awarded easy access to school resources such as guidance counselors, academic courses, recommendations for college, and ongoing publicity about their academic and athletic success and value for the school and community. High school principals are like politicians running for office who favor constituents who donate large sums to their election campaigns.

The difference in the consumer-driven school world is that these constituents of the principal are not giving financial donations for access, as donors do for politicians. Rather, their donations to the principal are the stories of their high level of achievement and success, which get translated into an ongoing sales campaign to sell the role of the principal and his school. It's a full-time job that gets replayed every school year. This salesperson role is among many other full-time jobs such as overseeing budgeting, discipline, curriculum development, and student athletic programs.

Inexperienced new principals learn early on this is a key role that comes with the title High School Principal. For ex-teachers and ex-counselors, it's not an easy transition. Many high school principals first go into teaching because they have a calling to help young people achieve and be successful. These future administrators often were guided by caring teachers and administrators as students, and they chose a career in education as a way to repay this gift.

However, entering the role of high school principal often takes them away from a face-to-face helping role with students. For some principals, being an administrator is more like having a corporate job than being useful to students. They often miss the joy, and sometimes turbulence and chaos, at the center of high school students' lives. It's not an easy role to adjust to for compassionate and caring educators.

Going from a caring educator to a role as a politician and a salesperson always in search of good news can be a big stretch. But they soon realize what the job is all about: seize the bully pulpit to herald success or be gone. Like the good news parents and bad news parents, they learn the tough lesson of what it means to be careful what you ask for. There may be unintended consequences waiting in the shadows for you.

One of those unintended consequences is that high school principals are being forced into the new role of chief marketer for their school. An increase in budget cuts, competition with charter schools for students, and overemphasis on the bad news that undermines public support have all forced high school principals to serve as chief salespersons to showcase their students' success and help local school budgets. Many high schools have a cadre of students who are very successful in academics, athletics, music, and theater and are highly visible performing community service.

They are star students who have amassed a portfolio of contributions to their school and community. The principal can easily mine these star students' portfolios and market their value to their community, parents, and school staff. In this marketing process, these high-achieving students, the good news kids, become a brand that people can rally around, a brand that offers hope to communities in difficult times when budget cuts and deteriorating support for public schools are on the increase.

But the selling of star students has a downside. The brand creates a college-bound, all-good-news culture that sidesteps or hides the stigma created by the bad news kids who are a given part of any high school culture. The principal's role in this marketing process—showcasing only a special section of his student body—tends to limit his role as principal for all his students.

In this college-bound culture, the benefits flow exclusively to the students who receive a particular education. These star students have worked hard to acquire marketable tokens of accomplishment such as high test scores, good grades, advanced placement, and academic credits. And for their hard work and effort to be positive examples of student life, they want, even demand, rewards—rewards a principal is able to offer in return for their serving as "instruments of gain" for the school.

For example, principals might advise guidance counselors to give top priority to counseling good news kids and their parents, ask academic teachers to funnel every bit of good news to the community, request that athletic coaches highlight the success of star athletes, ask teachers in the arts to chronicle their outstanding students' performances, and encourage community service and other club leaders to identify the wonderful work of good news kids.

By their actions, not by what they say, principals find themselves trapped in a marketing role that is narrowly focused on good news and leaves the rest of the school community, students, parents, and teachers as observers. It's a culture in which the best and brightest students and parents are treated as the most-valued customers. They represent the best of the product the school has to offer. Rafaela Espinal, principal of Public School 125 in New York City, says, "We have to think about selling ourselves all the time."[1] However, as Johnny E. Brooks reminds us, the public schools ought not to be selling and promoting themselves in ways designed to gloss over a tarnished image,[2] or to gloss over the lives of kids who have the potential to create a tarnished image, good news kids as well as bad news kids. Anyone can falter and suddenly find themselves at the margins of school and community life.

High school graduation ceremonies in which senior class members are celebrated for earning their diplomas are in fact showcases for the achievements of good news kids and their parents. While the name of every graduating senior is listed in the graduation program, the focus is on the contributions of these star students to the school and community.

Here's how the show is orchestrated in many communities. First there are comments by the president of the board of education, the superintendent of schools, and the high school principal. While the board president and superintendent talk generally about the achievements of the high-achieving class members, it is the high school principal's role, as marketing chief, to lay out the specific achievements of the good news kids; for example, the elite colleges they will be attending, their scholarships and awards, and how the achievements of these good news kids have had a positive impact on their school and community.

The high school principal knows how to bring good news kids and their parents into the show by asking them to stand and be applauded by the attendees. The contributions of these good news kids are usually listed in the graduation program, which again lists the colleges of choice, scholarships, and awards.

As for the bad news kids who were able to survive and make it to graduation, there is no college, scholarship, or award listed beside their name, only a citation stating, "Work" or "Army, Navy, Air Force, Marines."

This showcase illuminates how far the present-day high school culture is from Michael Sandel's observation that "democracy does not require perfect equality, but it does require citizens to share a common life. What matters is that people of different background and social positions encounter one another, and bump up against one another, in the course of everyday life. For this is how we learn to negotiate and abide our differences, and how we come to care for the common good."[3]

Graduation day is not a day on which students of different backgrounds and social positions encounter one another and share in a common life. It's a day honoring those who have learned the important lesson in consumer-driven schooling: get ahead and stay ahead.

And the director of this show is the high school principal. It's not a role he chose or coveted, and he may in private disparage it, for serving as marketer-in-chief keeps him from sharing in a common life with all his students. This role as chief marketer, a full-time job in itself, keeps him from encountering bad news kids and parents from different backgrounds and social positions in the course of his everyday professional role. Salespeople can't afford to waste their time on students and parents who are not "instruments of gain." There's no sale there. These students and parents have no tokens to offer.

Graduation day is not the place where tarnished images get exposed. It's a day that focuses on perfection, good-news stories, and how the best and brightest are raking in the cash and awards by putting their school and community on the map as a place where kids can learn how to get ahead and stay ahead. It's just another day in the life of a principal for whom selling the school 24 hours a day, 365 days a year, is his top priority as well as the top priority of his counselors and academic teachers.

The role of high school principal is best characterized as one of having "too much to do." And there are few "superprincipals" capable of being successful in all the essentials tasks required in their work. Something has to give. David Dunaway suggests as much in his article "Myth of the Super-Principal."[4]

Dunaway suggests that in every principal's experiences, a typical day is composed of a series of fifteen-minute problem-solving segments interspersed with interruptions of tragedy, hilarity, anger, and noise. In the middle of all of this, the principal is expected to set the vision of the school, increase parental engagement, know the names of all the students, know the birthdays of the children of faculty members, know the number of students on free and reduced lunch by sex and ethnicity, and be able to recite the statistics of the leading scorers from last night's boys and girls basketball games.

The principal is expected to develop strategies for increasing test performance, convince facility members who have little desire to solve school problems that they should help solve them and enjoy doing it, protect the constitutional rights of every student, and be able to quote special education law, chapter and verse. Add to this the time required for teacher observations, with pre- and post-conferences, and the hours required to write up these observations. Just the paperwork associated with the evaluation routines for a large faculty is astonishing.

One also must not forget that the principal is expected to be at every athletic event and club meeting and to participate in the civic life of the community after the school day is over. And being a model parent with a model family life is another community expectation. To these expectations add the paperwork required by the central office and staying up to date on the latest instructional materials, teaching methodologies, and discipline strategies. With the increasing emphasis on responding to e-mail and telephone messages promptly, some school systems are beginning to measure the response time from when a parent makes a request and that request is answered.

Dunaway reports that Robert W. Hetzel wrote in 1992, "Principals face a variety of tasks in an environment where the normal length of interaction or activity ranges from two to three minutes, and less than 15 percent of all tests last more than nine minutes." One might ask if anything has changed since 1992 to improve this situation. Unfortunately, it has only gotten worse. And one cannot be surprised to find that a focus on the knowable managerial aspects of the job too often takes precedence over the much less predictable and inherently more risky aspects of focusing on the core leadership function of the principalship: improving teaching and learning. Thus has been perpetrated on unsuspecting school leaders the myth of the superprincipal.

And the essential tasks of high school principals can be daunting. Here's a list of "essential tasks" for the job of high school principal in the Virginia Beach City public schools.[5]

Principal, Senior High School
General Responsibility
The position is responsible for the leadership, administration and supervision of high school and its programs.
Essential Tasks
(These are intended only as illustrations of the various types of work performed. The omission of specific duties does not exclude them from the position if the work is similar, related, or a logical assignment to the position.)

- Develop and maintain an effective educational program consistent with the State and Federal guidelines and the philosophy, policies, regulations and strategic plan of the School Board; maintain records and files; meet and confer with students, parents, faculty and staff.
- Establish a professional learning culture through a solid foundation of shared mission, vision, values and goals.
- Develop a collaborative culture for improving student achievement.
- Establish and maintain an effective learning climate in the school.
- Initiate, design and implement programs to meet specific needs of the school.
- Ensure implementation of the Virginia Beach Public Schools approved curriculum.
- Direct and monitor the development of the school's instructional program.
- Ensure the development of 21st century skills with all students.
- Plan, organize, and direct implementation of all school activities.
- Make recommendations concerning the school's administration and instruction.
- Assist with the preparation of the school's budget and monitor expenditures.
- Prepare or supervise the preparation of reports, records, lists and all other required information and data.
- Coordinate and work with the central administrative staff on school needs, problems, and/or effectiveness.

- Assume responsibility for the implementation and observance of all School Board policies and regulations by the school's staff and students; interpret and enforce school divisions policies and regulations.
- Schedule classes within established guidelines to meet students' needs.
- Assist in the development, revision, and evaluation of the curriculum.
- Supervise the guidance program.
- Monitor all dimensions of the special education program in the school to ensure compliance with federal, state, and local mandates and guidelines.
- Monitor the student Support Team process to ensure appropriate and timely interventions for students and subsequent referrals for other services if needed.
- Maintain high standards of student conduct and enforce discipline, as necessary, according to School Board policy and the due process rights of students.
- Attend special events held to recognize student achievement; attend school-sponsored activities, functions and athletic events.
- Maintain and control the various local funds generated by student activities.
- Supervise the maintenance of accurate records on the progress and attendance of students.
- Supervise all professional, paraprofessional, administrative, and non-professional personnel assigned to the school.
- Develop leadership skills, particularly instructional leadership, of the assistant principals assigned to the school.
- Participate in the selection of all school building personnel.
- Evaluate and counsel all staff members regarding their individual and group performance.
- Supervise the daily use of the school facilities for both academic and nonacademic purposes.
- Supervise and evaluate all activities and programs that are outgrowths of the school's curriculum.
- Perform related work as required.

A look at the essential tasks of a high school principal in the Virginia Beach public schools confirms our assessment that the current role of high school principals is a daunting task. This assessment is also supported by a Public Agenda report, "Rolling Up Their Sleeves: Superintendents and Principals Talk about What's Needed to Fix Public Schools."[6] The report suggests educational leaders are being asked to do more, much more, with fewer resources. Getting by with less is the name of the game in today's school world.

As a result, the report suggests a lot of the essential tasks of secondary school principals are not focused on their most important work: educating students. It should come as no surprise that high school principals are being forced into a marketing role to help ensure that school budgets are passed. As this book suggests, there are costs to students who are not a part of a college-bound culture in which the benefits flow exclusively to those students who receive a particular education and have highly marketable tokens they can use to acquire the most expert services a school can provide to get ahead and stay ahead. Here are some key elements of the Public Agenda report.

With public schools racked by state and local budget crises, it is hardly surprising that principals and superintendents consider money to be their number one problem. Creating reliable budgets for complex organizations is never easy; meeting the bottom line is always rough; today's economy is sluggish; and taxpayers can be a notoriously cranky and unappreciative lot even in much brighter economic times. Money is a big problem for school leaders, and they don't hesitate to say so.

But just beneath the surface of their money concerns is one aspect they find especially galling: the cost of obeying state and federal laws that require them to put very specific services or policies in place. According to school leaders, there are far too many of these mandates. They come in regularly from federal, state, and local governments. Most don't come with sufficient funding, and even when the money is there, the mandates are often abstruse, time-consuming, and out of sync with laws and regulations already on the books.

Asked to choose the most pressing issue facing their district, 70 percent of superintendents and 58 percent of principals say it is "insufficient school funding." By contrast, mere handfuls say "poor teacher quality" or a "lack of strong and talented administrators" is their top problem. One in 5 superintendents (20 percent) and 1 in 3 principals (33 percent) choose "implementation of the No Child Left Behind Act" as their major challenge, although lack of adequate funding is one of the major complaints school leaders have about the law.

Moreover, school leaders say, money problems are more severe than in the past. The number of school leaders who say funding is their top problem has risen in recent years, and 85 percent of superintendents and 80 percent of principals say the situation in their own district has gotten worse. In fact, 27 percent of superintendents and 23 percent of principals say lack of funding is such a critical problem in their district that only minimal progress can be made. Yet, as perhaps further evidence of their "can do" spirit, nearly 7 in 10 school leaders (68 percent of superintendents and 68 percent of principals) say "lack of funding is a problem but [they] can make progress given what [they] have."

There are big winners and losers in this dire "doing-more-with-less" scenario. The good news kids and parents are the winners. They are able to maintain their get-ahead, stay-ahead path because school districts need their good-news stories to pass budgets at a time when many parents want cutbacks such as reduced staff and zero pay increases. The good news kids and parents demand that school leaders stay away from cutting back academic teachers and college counselors who provide them with the benefits and access to school resources that can open up doors for them. Good news students and parents are the untouchables when it comes to cutting staff and programs.

However, being "special" can have its costs. For example, David McCullough, a long-time English teacher at Wellesley High School in Massachusetts, warned the school's 2012 graduates about the folly of being treated as "special" and thinking of oneself as "special." Here are some of the highlights of his speech "You Are Not Special. You Are Not Exceptional."[7]

> And now you've conquered high school . . . now, indisputably, here we all have gathered for you, the pride and joy of this fine community, the first to emerge from that magnificent new building. But do not get the idea you're anything special. Because you're not it.
>
> You see, if everyone is special, then no one is. If everyone gets a trophy, trophies become meaningless. In our unspoken but not so subtle Darwinian competition with one another, which springs, I think, from our fear of our own insignificance, a subset of our dread of mortality, we have of late, we Americans, to our detriment, come to love accolades more than genuine achievement.
>
> We have come to see them as the point and we're happy to compromise standards, or ignore reality, if we suspect that's the quickest way, or only way,

to have something to put on the mantelpiece, something to pose with, crow about, something with which to leverage ourselves into a better spot on the social totem pole. No longer is it how you play the game, no longer is it even whether you win or lose, or learn or grow, or enjoy yourself doing it . . . Now it's "So what does this get me?"

As a consequence, we cheapen worthy endeavors. . . . It's an epidemic and in its way not even dear old Wellesley High is immune . . . one of the best of the 37,000 nationwide. Wellesley High School . . . where good is no longer good enough, where a B is the new C, and the midlevel curriculum is called Advanced College Placement. And I hope you caught me when I said, "One of the best."

I said, "One of the best" so we can feel better about ourselves, so we can bask in a little easy distinction, however vague and unverifiable, and count ourselves among the elite, whoever they might be, and enjoy a perceived leg up on the perceived competition. But the phrase defies logic. By definition there can be only one best. You're it or you're not.

Commenting after his speech, Mr. McCullough said, "So many of the adults around them, the behavior of adults around them, gives them this sort of inflated sense of themselves. And I thought they needed a little context, a little perspective. To send them off into the world with an inflated sense of themselves is doing them no favor."

The other loser in consumer-driven schools such as Wellesley is the high school principal who must maintain the facade of being a principal for every student while in fact his role is to use the good news kids and parents to help save his school and staff, including staff members from non-academic departments such as music, art, business, technology, and theater who are often the first to be let go, furloughed, or sent to another school when staff cutbacks are called for. They are the dispensable ones, not the academic teachers who are indispensable to the success of good news kids.

And the bad news kids and their parents are big losers. The divide between them and the good news kids and parents gets bigger as school districts are forced to get along with less. Teachers in the non-academic courses they take such as math, science, English, and social studies are also on the list of teachers who are dispensable when staff cutbacks are forced on the high school principal.

These teachers have no place in the more-valued world of academic teachers nor do the bad news kids they teach. They are both dispensable. They don't travel in the same circles as academic teachers and good news kids. They don't encounter one another and bump up against one another in the course of everyday life. So when non-academic teachers are let go and bad news kids drop out, the high school's focus on good news kids and parents doesn't waiver. It's akin to shrugging your shoulders and mouthing the right words such as "We'll miss you." However, these teachers and kids are soon forgotten, their place in the school soon erased by the ongoing good-news stories.

The public schools, in particular high schools, need a more democratic assessment of how "every" student views his or her school's contribution to his or her own quality of life while a student and not just reports about the achievements and accolades of star students. This sad tale is not the doing of caring principals who entered the role of principal to help kids and teachers be all they could be. They are caught up in the get-ahead, stay-ahead world, as are counselors for the college bound and academic teachers who give out the tokens needed to help good news kids gain entrance into elite colleges. It's a world in which the get-ahead, stay-ahead crowd is favored, and the rest be damned.

McCullough is on to our bifurcated system. It's an epidemic in which the get-ahead, stay-ahead, "so what does this get me?" crowd is pushing harder and harder, and caring principals wonder how to change this rampant love for accolades while knowing that these accolades may be saving the jobs of many of their teachers and maybe their own when it comes time to pass the yearly school budget. It is a role in which many high school principals feel they are being torn apart by powerful forces. Do they go along to get along? Or do they choose to give up their chief marketing role and risk the consequences?

New York Times columnist Thomas L. Friedman[8] suggests leaders would be better off if they told people the truth. Friedman refers to the advice of Don Seidman, author of the book *How: Why How We Do Anything Means Everything . . . in Business (and in Life)*, who has long argued that "nothing inspires people more than the truth." Most leaders think that telling people the truth makes that leader vulnerable to the public or their opponents. They are wrong.

Seidman says, "The most important part of telling the truth is that it actually binds you to people because when you trust people with the truth, they trust you back. Trusting people with the truth is like giving them a solid floor. It compels action. When you are anchored in shared truth, you start to solve problems together. It's the beginning of coming up with a better plan."

As Wellesley's David McCullough's commencement speech suggests, there may be value in Seidman's advice to "tell the truth." McCullough's speech alerted students, educators, parents, and citizens that all was not well in their get-ahead, stay-ahead, consumer-driven school culture. Yet it appears this wake-up call was not met with open arms by many parents and citizens. No doubt it was too close to home for the comfy, entrenched, "so what does this get me?" crowd.

But McCullough's speech has value. The speech served to expose an educational system designed to reward and benefit "special" students and parents. As a result, it served to open up a conversation for school communities throughout America on the question, Whose school is it? A school just for "special" students, or a school for "all" students, as they are all "special"?

NOTES

1. Jenifer Medina, "Pressed by Charters, Public Schools Try Marketing," www.nytimes.com/2010/03/10 (accessed June 20, 2012).

2. Johney Brooks, "Marketing the Public Schools," *Education Leadership* 40, no. 11 (1982): 22–24.

3. Michael J. Sandel, *What Money Can't Buy: The Moral Limits on Money* (New York: Farrar, Straus and Giroux, 2012).

4. David Dunaway, "Myth of the Super Principal," http://cnx.org/content/m20832/latest/ (accessed July 1, 2012).

5. Virginia Beach Public Schools, "Essential Tasks, Principal, Senior High School," www.vbschools.com.hr/job-desc/principal%20hs.pdf (accessed July 8, 2012).

6. Public Agenda, "Rolling Up Their Sleeves: Superintendents and Principals Talk about What's Needed to Fix Public Schools," *Public Agenda* (2003): 11–12, 16–17, 45–46.

7. B. Brown, "Wellesley High Grads Told: You're Not Special," www.theswellesleyreport.com/2012/06/wellesley-high-grads-told-youre-not-special (accessed June 30, 2012).

8. Thomas L. Friedman, "The Rise of Popularism," *New York Times*, June 24, 2012.

Chapter Five

The Cost to Guidance Counselors

There are star guidance counselors just like there are star students. They are professionals who are known on the school and community grapevine as the go-to persons for the college bound. However, these star counselors are not really counselors who are trained and committed to helping teens navigate the perils of high school life or simply plan for what happens after high school life has ended.

Rather, these star counselors are the data collectors, managers, and script writers for the good news kids' success stories—stories that are funneled to the principal to be used in marketing the school's success to community members, staff, and students. Counselors are ideally positioned for this role as they oversee counseling for college-bound students, provide them with information on scholarship and awards, and use their connections with college admissions personnel to sell their best and brightest star students. The good news kids are given top priority. The parents of these star students are also given top priority, with 24/7 access when questions arise.

In this role, guidance counselors are actually quasi-administrators. While many were trained to offer personal counseling intervention for troubled students and parents, once they arrive on the high school campus they quickly learn personal counseling is not a top priority. Instead, it's all about getting students into college, counseling them on how to win awards and financial aid, and how to take the necessary courses and get the necessary social experiences to build a great resume.

Meanwhile, the bad news kids, who are in need of personal counseling and intervention to help redirect their lives, are not in the mix. If lucky, they may find a caring teacher, coach, or community advocate to guide them. If not, their path is usually one of failure, absenteeism, and dropping out. Most of those who do make it to graduation do it on their own, but they are in the minority.

Since their beginning in the 1950s, the high school guidance and counseling programs that were designed to offer every student access to personal, academic, and career counseling have instead become an arm of the school administration, overseeing college admissions, mandated testing, and scheduling, and accessing positive data from these programs to identify and report good-news stories. Today's high school guidance directors often hold the title of Guidance Director and Data Manager.

Guidance counselors then are the school's managers in charge of finding students who are "instruments of gain and objects of use." They are a guiding light in helping star students, as David McCullough suggests, "have something to put on the mantelpiece, something to pose with, crow about, something with which to leverage [themselves] into a better spot on the social totem pole."[1] They are the professionals who are there to answer star students when they ask, "So what does this get me?"—an obvious question when star students and their parents consider which courses to take, which activities will help them shine to get ahead and stay ahead, and what accolades they can expect to come their way.

Good news kids and parents, and guidance counselors themselves, love accolades because it helps create the persona of a doer and shaker. As McCullough says of star students, "smiles ignite when you walk into a room, and hundreds gasp with delight at your every tweet."[2] Today's guidance counselors can also quietly bask in the limelight as they see their star protégés walk down the runway, knowing they made it all happen. In today's high schools, most guidance counselors and good news kids and parents are in it together, all reaping the benefits and accolades that flow to high achievers.

In this system, counselors who are trained to offer personal counseling become easily transformed into quasi-administrators responsible for counseling students for classes, discipline, college admissions, etc. These are the activities that counselors soon learn to be successful at in order to keep their job as key members of the school's bureaucracy. Resisting this quasi-administrative role can cost counselors their job. They also soon learn that they are not really responsible or expected to offer personal counseling to students. As one high school counselor reports,

It's not a priority really for our counselors.

If it happens, fine, but the job is all about increasing the numbers of kids being assigned to classes in which they can succeed, increasing the test scores and college admission number, and decreasing the number of discipline problems and absentees. I was trained in grad school to provide intervention and group counseling, but that's not what my job is all about. I've become a paper pusher and see my dream of helping kids being buried under a pile of paper.

The school is only interested in my numbers for what I call the big five; scheduling, college admissions, testing, career counseling, and discipline. No one cares about how many kids I see for personal counseling because it's not a priority. And believe me, if I am seen spending too much time seeing kids for personal counseling and ignoring my big administrative duties, I'll be in big trouble. Got to go along to get along is what this job is all about.

As this counselor painfully points out, the personal counseling of students gets relegated to a low priority. In many schools, no one in leadership is asking counselors for the number of students they are seeing for personal counseling, and, as a result, counselors realize it's not a priority. They keep up with their administrative responsibilities because that's the ticket to tenure and survival. Guidance programs have become a vehicle to "sell" the school's brand to school boards, parents, tax payers, parents, and even to the school itself as proof that it is a successful and winning institution. Passing budgets is the driving force behind the work of today's school counselors.

Meanwhile, you don't hear school superintendents speaking at high school graduations about the number of students receiving personal counseling intervention. What you usually hear is how many students were accepted to college, how many scholarships and financial awards were received, and the names of students who excelled in academics as well as sports, music, art, drama, etc. The focus is on students who are high achievers and who bring ongoing media attention to themselves and the school.

One could say that secondary schools ride the successes of these high achievers as "the" vehicle to pass school budgets. As such, high achievers demand and get the guidance services they need to compete for admission to competitive colleges, win scholarships, and be anointed as standard-bearers carrying the flag of success for their school and the community. The guidance program in many schools is geared to managing the good news and helping create a positive spin, with the goal of making sure bad news gets buried.

However, the good-news-only approach comes with a high cost that is often overlooked and can serve to derail the main mission of a caring school:

educating and guiding every student to be all he or she can be. In this good-news-only world, troubled teens need to look elsewhere for help. Many are not newsmakers whose activities and successes support their school's positive profile. They are simply kids looking for a caring, welcoming adult who can provide them with a trusting, safe place, a place where they can forge a new plan for their lives. Their story is not a good-news story filled with many successes. However, it is a story they know needs changing, with a hope for a new beginning. But for many, the help they need has eluded them so far.

It is true that one size doesn't fit all guidance counselors, and there are counselors who would prefer a personal counseling role helping both good news kids and bad news kids with their many personal issues. However, they often find themselves limited to advocating for the good news kids and their success stories. They are like medical doctors who have been trained to be psychiatrists but are put in charge of a billing department. They have the training, degrees, and skills to be leaders of an intervention effort, but no one is asking for their participation.

The perks for guidance counselors are aligned with the get-ahead, stay-ahead crowd. Successfully guiding the best and brightest students to achieve high grades, good test scores, scholarships, awards, and entrance into top-rated colleges brings with it a counselor's own brand of parent, student, and community appreciation and accolades. Like their high-achieving students, they too become "somebody" of importance in the school and in the community.

And many of guidance counselors' achievements as "facilitators of success" come via their connections to college admissions directors. They are wined and dined by admissions officers at national, state, and local conferences and college fairs.

The reality is that many members of the higher education community see guidance counselors as their ticket to maintaining their student enrollment, and they are increasing their wooing approach. College admissions directors want guidance counselors focused on guiding high school students to their colleges, not spending time solving personal problems. And they continuously work at shoring up with perks this image of the counselor's role.

Staff writer Gregg Winter describes the wooing process used by college admissions directors such as Victor I. Davolt of Regis University, located in Denver, Colorado.[3] Winter reports that for the past two years, Davolt has played host to high school guidance counselors, the "extremely influential" people he hopes will send more students to his ninety-acre campus. He flies them in from around the country to meet the faculty and review the curriculum, but he also includes skiing on the world-famous slopes of Vail, snowmobiling, spending time at a spa, and getting a facial or massage, all courtesy of the university. Further, Davolt treats counselors to professional hockey games and rooms at luxury hotels. Winter observes that although the image of the admissions process is often one of high school counselors buttering up colleges in hopes of gaining an advantage for their students, the reality is sometimes the other way around.

Colleges are so intent on getting not just enough applicants but the best ones that lavishing perks on guidance counselors has become a priority for admissions personnel. For example, when the admissions staff at Center City College in Danville, Kentucky, invites guidance counselors to visit, it puts them up in a bed and breakfast and takes them golfing at a country club and to a racetrack. It even gives them a small stake, around fifty dollars, so they can gamble on the horses. Goucher College in Towson, Maryland, takes visiting counselors to the theater, the symphony, and Baltimore Orioles games and rents out the Rock and Roll Hall of Fame for a night to thank counselors.

Ralph S. Figueroa, director of college guidance at Albuquerque Academy, a private school in New Mexico, suggests, "We can't help but be swayed by the people who are nice to us, who buy nice things for us." These college excursions offer short-term but tangible rewards for guidance counselors in that they provide an open door through which they can escape from their often hectic school life, which can include dealing with critics, and instead be wined and dined and made to feel they are needed.

However, even with their elevated position in the get-ahead, stay-ahead, "so what does this get me?" school culture, counselors are steadily reminded that this role is top priority, and they need to keep their personal counseling with kids to a minimum. The pressure to not stray into a personal counselor role never ends. A report from the Education Trust[4] puts the preferred role to counsel the best and brightest students in stark reality.

The report, "Posed to Lead: How School Counselors Can Drive College and Career Readiness," is very critical of one aspect of counselors' work. The report states the counselors themselves can diminish their scope of influence. For example, the report states that, in a misguided effort, too many counselors allow students to drop rigorous courses or, worse, never enroll in them. Unfortunately, this "bless-your-heart" mentality results in choices that slam the door on those students' futures. This is quite different from excusing them from doing hard work, a practice that has devastating repercussions in limiting students' life options.

The report hits hardest with its criticism of counselors who put an overemphasis on personal counseling. For example, the report states that even school counselors who have high expectations for their students can easily find themselves spending the bulk of their time providing personal and social counseling to individual students.

The report also suggests that school counselors mean well with these efforts, but the hard truth is that our public schools are not set up to provide therapy to students. Certainly, when personal and social issues significantly interfere with learning, school counselors need to help. They can best assist students not with long-term, time-consuming sessions, but with brief, short-term counseling sessions, referrals to small-group counseling, and other support systems within the school or community.

As a result, in most large high schools, counselors have little out-of-the-office time to know all their students; to observe them in class, in the hallways, at lunch, and during activities; and to be a positive presence in the school, a presence through which the counselor will know each student well and the students know him well, creating an opportunity for positive connections established by ongoing personal contact.

That's not the case in many of our large, overcrowded high schools. Counselors are locked in their offices trying to figure out how to reduce discipline and suspension rates, and ways to improve attendance, test scores, graduation and post-secondary enrollment rates, and staff morale at a time when teachers are continually being asked to do more with less and to sell their school to a negative public.

As a result, these counselors are often isolated from the school world and miss out on the positive things that are happening with their students, staff, and parents. They can document and herald the percentages of students who are becoming better achievers, but they receive far too few real stories about students at the margins of school life.

The cost to high school counselors is both personal and professional in their consumer-driven school culture. The professional cost comes from being channeled into a counseling role focused on serving the best and brightest students. It's a quasi-administrative role with one goal in mind: helping the most successful students get ahead and stay ahead. However, in this limited and isolating role, high school counselors have little involvement with bad news kids and their parents.

Over time they begin to value the good news kids and parents more because they offer little resistance and early on learn how to play the game of "what's in it for me?" They are nice, well-behaved, motivated. They know how to say, "Thank you so much, Sir," and they are easy to counsel. These star students know how to sell counselors on what great kids they are and why the counselors need to help them—help them until they hit pay dirt with that college acceptance letter.

In this role, high school counselors can become set in their ways, and soft, because few challenges come their way if they know how to play the game of helping bright kids get ahead and stay ahead. They become soft in the sense that they rarely encounter bad news kids and parents, who are not nice, motivated, well-behaved, or interested in going along to get along. The bad news kids are not interested in sucking up to educators, counselors included. They often offer great resistance to educators in "offices" such as administrators, counselors, and psychologists. They understand they have no friends in high places so they put little faith in being "helped" by office types.

As a result, counselors often lose the ability, motivation, and skill to take on, confront, and help students who are not on the path to college, the bad news kids who make those who want to help them sweat and get angry, and who often are labeled as "not interested in being helped." However, as many educators will tell you, they often learn more from resistant kids who aren't interested in what they are selling. And these bad news kids make their position abundantly clear to would-be helpers who approach them by signaling, "You better be up to the challenge I am about to give you." "Show me your best stuff," as one student said.

So many high school counselors miss out on the professional and personal growth this experience could offer because of their limited, consumer-driven helping role as quasi-administrators, a role that is often a clerical role, managing data and public relations. It is also not a role focused on counseling of the whole child, centered on knowing each student well and helping the student become all he or she can be. They forget that all students are special in their own way and should not be viewed simply as "instruments of gain and objects of use."

This is not an easy culture and practice to change, but the change is a needed one if we are going to develop an alternative school culture in which students from every section of the school community connect with one another on a daily basis, get to know each other well, and rid themselves of the habit of seeing each other only as different, as not one of us, as "instruments of gain and objects of use." Knowing each other well is the basis of a successful, healthy, and supportive school community in which members who are faltering and at the margins of school life are offered help, a community in which members act, not turn away, when they see trouble visiting a member of the community: a student, teacher, administrator, member of the support staff, parent, or even counselor.

NOTES

1. B. Brown, "Wellesley High Grads Told: You're Not Special," www.theswellesleyreport.com/2012/06/wellesley-high-grads-told-youre-not-special (accessed June 30, 2012).

2. Brown, "Wellesley High Grads Told: You're Not Special."

3. Gregg Winter, "Wooing the Counselors Raises Enrollment and Also Eyebrows," *New York Times*, July 8, 2004, 1A, 18A.

4. The Education Trust, "Poised to Lead: How School Counselors Can Drive College and Career Readiness," *Education Trust* (December 2011): 2–6.

Chapter Six

The Cost to Teachers

There are star academic teachers just as there are star students. These star teachers are found in courses that attract the best and brightest, students, such as advanced placement classes and advanced courses in math, English, science, and social studies, as well as courses with college credit. Students who succeed in these classes and score a college recommendation are well placed to earn a spot in an elite college.

As such, these elite star teachers are treated with great respect by good news kids, good news parents, guidance counselors, and the school administration. These are the teachers who have the power to make good things happen for their students, such as coveted rewards and scholarships. They may not make more money than other senior teachers or have their own working place with a sign reading Elite Teachers Only, but they know their worth as a driving force in the success of their high-achieving students and their school. They are "teachers of great interest" as good news kids and parents vie for a place in their classes.

Not only is there a hierarchy among students, with good news kids ensconced at the very top, there is a hierarchy among teachers, with the elite academic teachers comfortably situated at the top and knowing, like their star students, that they represent the best and the brightest among their peers. The annual kudos awarded to these elite teachers at graduation time cements their vital role to the school and community as the doers who prepare high-achieving students to excel and find their chosen place in getting ahead and staying ahead.

These elite teachers know how to answer when star students ask, "So what does this get me?" and that answer is a first-class ticket out of here to a world where they will always be at the top rung. It is not always the truth, but a part of the rhetoric suggesting our best and brightest kids will never falter, given the training they've had by special teachers. These teachers are the special ones in schools where many teachers are seen as not special.

And the "not special" teachers are the teachers of the bad news kids and the students who are not college bound. These teachers, like their students, are not given accolades or special mention at graduation ceremonies or in school media promotions. They do not appear in pictures or special stories. They are the frontline troops trying to educate and reach troubled teens or teens who long ago gave up and are now warming a seat—uninvolved and seemingly uninterested, waiting for something to happen that might wake them from their passive roles.

These classrooms are difficult places, full of angry or passive students being taught by teachers who know that their place in the school hierarchy is at the bottom. Like the kids they teach and the parents they try to help, these teachers too know who gets the perks, benefits, and rewards in their school. They know they are not members, and never will be, of that club. They understand that's how the game of a consumer-driven school is played. These bad news teachers are mired, as are their students, in a daily battle for survival. Help and intervention is not on the way.

And they know that, being at the bottom, when hard times arrive and budget cuts are called for, they will often be the first to be asked to leave or to be transferred to another school where they will still be at the bottom, again the first ones to go. Divisions, hierarchy, and special treatment are not isolated to students in our high schools. The good news kids and their parents, star guidance counselors, and elite academic teachers are all in it together to garner benefits and accolades. They are in the club of privilege in the school, and their self-indulgent behavior lets the rest of the school population know who counts.

Make no doubt about it, there is a caste system in our high schools. The elite academic teachers and star guidance counselors are the Brahmins who have political clout and quietly rule their school. The teachers of bad news kids are the Sundras, the followers, who have no say. If staff parking spaces were assigned to Sundras teachers, they would probably be miles away, only reachable by a shuttle, the Sundras Shuttle!

In most high schools there is no collegial community of teachers. The elite teachers are reluctant to work collaboratively or to open their practice to others. It's their gig, and fellow staff members outside the cadre of academic elite teachers are not welcomed. "Don't ever try to play in my sandbox" is their mantra. As a result, there is no sense of community in which teachers have valued relationships with each other. Think of the Korean 49th parallel, the Berlin Wall, and Cuba when you view the divisions in our high schools. Warnings abound saying, "Don't invade the territory of elite teachers."

Elite teachers, like any successful salesperson, know how to attract the best and brightest students. Simply put, they own the good-news-kids brand, and collegiality and developing a sense of community seems irrelevant from their lofty perch in the school hierarchy and caste system. The special achievements of a cadre of good news students are the main source of pride for the school and community.

Elite academic teachers understand they are the doers and shakers responsible for this pride. They have higher status, greater respect, and more access to school resources. They enjoy a coveted role central to the school's success, compared to non-academic and vocational teachers who cope with students often labeled as "at-risk" and in need of remedial attention.

Morton Inger[1] suggests vocational and academic teachers are sustained by the value attached to the two different student bodies. The value placed on preparation of the college bound sets the standard, marginalizing the non–college bound and their teachers, who find themselves viewed by almost everyone in the school community as caretakers of marginal students.

In the high school culture, it's the elite academic teachers and star guidance counselors who have the winning ticket for public support while the vocational teachers find themselves in a losing, caretaker role, a role of trying to fix kids and parents who often have a long history of broken lives and of being marginalized in their school and community. These are the students who early on retreated from consumer-driven schooling. They are the truants, class cutters, tobacco smokers, and failures who understand they will never become "special" or be given the awards and accolades of good news kids. They are the kids and parents who have "no tokens" to enter their consumer-driven school.

In this consumer-driven schooling model, collegiality among staff is also a big loser because what counts is "what does this get me?" for good news kids, good news parents, elite academic teachers, and star guidance counselors. These live and operate in a school world that is isolated and structured to limit encounters with marginalized students, parents, and teachers—teachers who, like their students and their parents, have no tokens to gain benefits, rewards, or accolades and who remain as caretakers over their career.

So when education reformers suggest that greater collaboration among teachers is promising, don't bet the house on it. What the collaboration reformers are suggesting is a culture in which teachers open up their classroom doors, share a personal and professional relationship, look out for and help each other, and develop a supportive culture in which each teacher can be successful. Good stuff, but hardly the collaboration model now in place in our high schools.

The collaboration model now in place is not focused on developing a supportive culture in order to help each teacher be successful. Rather, it's a limited collaboration to help a privileged section of the school community get ahead and stay ahead. This is a collaboration of the chosen few who are recipients of the benefits, rewards, and accolades of consumer-driven schooling.

A better description of this "collaboration" would be a palace coup in which the so-called elite students, parents, and teachers have seized control and view the schoolhouse as serving their own personal and professional interests. It's not a democratic process in which each member of the school community is seen as "special" and as having something of value to contribute. Michael L. Sandel suggests that "democracy does not require perfect equality, but it does require that citizens share a common life."[2]

Maybe our present system cannot be changed and we are stuck with good news kids, their parents, and elite teachers and counselors reaping the reward of educational access and advantage. But in this process there is a big loss for elite teachers, as there is for good news kids and their parents, bad news kids and their parents, and the principals and guidance counselors whose role is to promote the system.

For elite teachers, the loss is never having the opportunity to teach, guide, and support students at the margins of school life, students who are not interested and are not prepared, who talk back, make mischief, and resist every effort by teachers to get them involved. These are the kind of students who "don't go along to get along," play the school game of "so what does this get me?" or kowtow to get a good grade.

These students have the ability to make teachers squirm and become uneasy, anxious, and hostile. They make teachers work hard, extra hard, to see if the teachers have within themselves the motivation, desire, and skills to help the students become successful learners. They can easily destroy a teacher of good news kids because they are not out to get ahead and stay ahead. They are out to see if the teacher has the courage to take them on, to be curious and interested in who they are as students, persons, and family members, and to value what they have to offer.

Interacting with hard-to-reach marginal kids and their parents can teach comfortable teachers how to leave their shell of comfort and risk being unnerved, anxious, and forced to develop new skills in the heat of the battleground classrooms they inhabit—a lesson elite teachers will never learn, being stuck in their comfortable cocoon surrounded by the fake praise of slobbering good news kids and their parents. The elite teacher's world holds little risk and little gain. These are teachers who have become "instruments of gain and objects of use" themselves and don't see the negative consequences of always helping good news kids get ahead, stay ahead, and find the path to "so what does this get me?"

For competent teachers, even the elite of their school, staying with what they know and playing it safe is, over time, a major block to their career development. Successful teachers, like successful athletes, musicians, actors, and dancers, need to live on the edge and avoid the hype, dazzle, and accolades that come with being a star and being greeted as a "somebody" when they walk into a room of admirers.

Elite teachers have a cocoon, a safety zone, around them that is filled with never-ending applause telling them how great they are. Being a star in the consumer-driven school can damage one's growth as a teacher. The safe cocoon that surrounds the elite teacher often drowns out the fear of extinction and insignificance and the fear of running out of the energy, ideas, and emotional gas that are key to growth.

A habit of living off the accolades of the ever-supportive and praising cast that is part of his or her daily routine can blind a star teacher to the risks that come with settling for the applause. Holding court and spreading wisdom among the good news flock can diminish one's ability to take risks and discover new approaches, particularly when the cast of good news kids and parents never changes and is always hungry to know how to get ahead and stay ahead.

However, a career of helping good news kids get ahead and stay ahead can be draining, even boring for star teachers. If the cocoon and safety zone that surrounds them is pierced ever so slightly, the question which often arises is, "What is the point of doing what you already know?" One has to adapt to succeed at the craft of teacher. One has to fight the sophistication, knowing, and boredom that comes with being a star teacher. These are the enemies of every teacher, including, surprisingly, star teachers who seem to have it all.

As the poet Anne Carson[3] suggests, "You don't learn anything when you are still on the window shelf, safe. The other way is to jump from what you know into an empty space and see where you end up. I think you only learn when you jump."

But it's hard to jump when the applause and the embrace of the good news crowd has you blocked in.

NOTES

1. Morton Inger, "Teacher Collaboration in Secondary Schools," http://voc.serve.berkeley.edu/centerfocus/cf2.html (accessed July 3, 2012).

2. Michael J. Sandel, *What Money Can't Buy: The Moral Limits on Money* (New York: Farrar, Straus and Giroux, 2012).

3. Melanie Rehak, "Things Fall Together," *New York Times*, March 26, 2000.

Chapter Seven

Schools Are Caught in a Bifurcation of American Society: Equal Opportunity Has Become a Forgotten Vision

Equal opportunity has become a forgotten vision for the bad news students and their parents, while the good news students and their parents, the privileged ones, continue their rapid climb to "take all" in the race for college and education, good jobs, and financial security. It's a dismal scenario in which schools are caught in carrying out programs that benefit their best and brightest students. But carrying out programs to give special students a leg up in garnering college acceptances, scholarships, and accolades has subtle costs as educators, particularly in high schools, find their schools being marginalized to aid the top tier of students and their families.

Strong forces in our society are at work to frame the mission of our schools as being primarily concerned with helping the standard-bearer be successful. The historic mission of the schools to foster equal opportunity has all but vanished except in the rhetoric of politicians and school leaders. Educators are living this sham each day and see their once important mission of creating equal opportunity for "all" students placed on the back burner.

David Brooks[1] accurately describes the forces that are at work and how our institutions are being manipulated to help widen the gap between college-bound, often affluent, kids and poorer kids who have little support, few advocates, and few opportunities to get ahead and stay ahead. In his article "The Opportunity Gap," Brooks calls on the research of Robert Putnam, who suggests our institutions, public schools included, are caught in a bifurcation of American society in which opportunities increasingly flow to college-bound students while poorer students are left with few open doors to get ahead.

Brooks reports that while most studies look at the inequality of outcomes among adults and help us understand how America is coming apart, Putnam's group looked at inequality of opportunities among children. This helps us understand what the country will look like in the decades ahead. The quick answer? More divided than ever.

Putnam's data verify what many of us have seen anecdotally: the children of the more affluent and the less affluent are raised in starkly different ways and have different opportunities. Decades ago, college-educated parents and high-school-educated parents invested similarly in their children. Recently, more-affluent parents have invested much more in their children's futures while less-affluent parents have not.

For example, more-affluent parents have invested more time. Over the past decades, college-educated parents have quadrupled the amount of time they spend reading *Goodnight Moon* to their kids, talking to their kids about their day, and cheering them on from the sidelines. High-school-educated parents have increased their child-care time, but only slightly.

A generation ago, working-class parents spent slightly more time with their kids than college-educated parents. Now college-educated parents spend an hour more every day. This attention gap is the largest in the first three years of life when it is most important.

Affluent parents also invest more money in their children. Over the past forty years, more-affluent parents have increased the amount they spend on their kids' enrichment activities, like tutoring, by $5,300 a year. The financially stressed less-affluent classes have only been able to increase their investment by $480, adjusted for inflation.

As a result, behavior gaps are opening up. In 1972, kids from the bottom quartile of earners participated in roughly the same number of activities as kids from the top quartile. Today, it's a chasm. Richer kids are roughly twice as likely to play after-school sports. They are more than twice as likely to be the captains of their sports team. They are much more likely to do non-sporting activities, like theater, the school yearbook, and Scouting. They are much more likely to attend religious services.

It's not only that richer kids have become more active. Poorer kids have become more pessimistic and detached. Social trust has fallen among all income groups, but between 1975 and 1995, it plummeted among the poorest third of young Americans and has remained low ever since. Putnam writes in notes prepared for the Aspen Ideas Festival, "It's perfectly understandable that kids from working-class backgrounds have become cynical and even paranoid, for virtually all our major social institutions have failed them—family, friends, church, school and community."

As a result, poorer kids are less likely to participate in voluntary service work that might give them a sense of purpose and responsibility. Their test scores are lagging. Their opportunities are more limited. Brooks concludes that a long series of cultural, economic, and social trends have merged to create this sad state of affairs. Traditional social norms have been abandoned, meaning more children are born out of wedlock. Their single parents simply have less time and fewer resources to prepare them for a more competitive world. Working-class jobs have been decimated, meaning that many parents are too stressed to have the energy, time, or money to devote to their children.

Affluent, intelligent people are more likely to marry other energetic, intelligent people. They raise energetic, intelligent kids in self-segregated, cultural ghettoes where they know little about and have less influence upon people who do not share their blessings.

As reported in chapter 1, David F. Labaree suggests in his book *Someone Has to Fail* that "consumers—the families who send children to school, have wanted schools to allow them to accomplish goals that are . . . more resonant personally: to get ahead and stay ahead."[2] They are "families trying to fortify the future of their children through the medium of schooling. In short, the vision of education as a private good (formed by the self-interested actions of individual consumers) has consistently won out over education as a public good (formed by the social aims of reform movements)."

Labaree argues, in contrast with school reformers, that consumers are less interested in the vocational skills that schools can provide than in the occupational doors schools can open. Access to a good job and a secure social position are their main concerns, and school is the way to gain these ends.

In this consumer-driven education model, the school system is focused on "credentialing" more than on learning, and the benefits flow to the degree holders. The students who fail, the bad news kids, are at the margins of school life and lack the support, resources, and motivation to get ahead and stay ahead. They are relegated to a vocational curriculum which has lower value than that of the college-bound students who are enrolled in a particular level of education that offers these students an advantage for jobs, an advantage not enjoyed by the bad news students.

Schools are good at assigning labels that certify students at higher or lower levels of merit. A wise observer from the world of gambling might say, "This game is rigged in favor of the good news kids and parents." To these consumer-driven students and their parents, what students learn in the classroom is irrelevant; what matters is whether they have acquired a form of educational currency, a diploma, which they can cash in for a good job. What is most salient about schooling for them is not its value, what usable knowledge it provides, but its exchange value, what doors it will open up.

On the surface this seems to be a success story for a few members of the school community, the good news kids and their parents, and a failing story—someone has to fail—for the bad news kids and their parents. However, a closer look at this consumer-driven school world reveals there are many other members of the school community who are failing in the schools' mission to educate every child and help them become all they can be. Not only are principals, guidance counselors, elite star teachers, and teachers of marginal students failing, so are good news students and their parents and marginalized bad news students and their parents.

Star students, their parents and elite teachers, and their guidance counselors appear to be very successful, but they too are part of a losing scenario because the consumer-driven path they follow is all about helping them get ahead and stay ahead but lacks interest, concern, and any welcome for other members of the school community. They are self-promoters filled with only their own interests.

However, as this book suggests, they may soon learn the hard lesson that in life we may lose or miss an important part of who we are, what we want to become, and what we stand for in the pursuit of our own personal gains. We may be known as leaders for all our achievements, rewards, and accolades, but in fact we have become only leaders for Number One: ourselves.

Consumer-driven education has supplanted the democratic mission of institutions such as the public schools in which, as Michael Sandel suggests, what matters is that people of different backgrounds and social positions encounter one another in the course of everyday life.[3] But for now and the near future, Sandel's hopeful vision is on hold. The forces that are compelling school leaders, star guidance counselors, and elite academic teachers to promote the credentialing of high-achieving students are in charge. They have won the battle for access and advantage, and consumer-driven schooling is the law of the land. But the battle has left many scarred victims. According to David Brooks, and as verified by Robert Putnam's research, it's an alarming and horrifying picture.

A long series of cultural, economic, and social trends have merged to create this sad state of affairs. The good news, if any, for educators is that Putnam's research might increase our awareness that we, as a country and as educators, are not taking advantage of all the country's human capital and instead are taking advantage of the capital of just the country's most privileged members.

If educators come to realize that their reason for becoming an educator, to help their students be all they can be, has been high-jacked by the get-ahead, stay-ahead crowd, they might, at the least, make an effort to connect with the bad news kids and their parents and be their advocate once in a while. Venturing across the tracks into unfamiliar territory can lead to finding gems.

They might also caution the good kids and their parents that focusing their lives totally on getting ahead may deprive them of the once-in-a-lifetime opportunity to just be a kid and hang out and not be burdened by deadline after deadline or have to resort to using pills to stay ahead. Small acts of kindness that connect kids and parents from different corners of the school culture can increase social trust, helping them to learn how to care for the common good, how to treat each other as persons worthy of dignity and respect, and how to restore the mission of equal opportunity to our public schools, in particular our high schools.

Our society and schools have much to lose if we fail to break down the barriers that are limiting the opportunities for our bad news kids. Marian Wright Edelman suggests that giving all children an education still benefits an entire community, and not educating children still makes it more likely their futures of "ignorance and vices" will cost us dearly in their consequences.[4]

Edelman reports that, for many years, teachers remained deeply respected for being strong positive role models for children who otherwise might not have positive role models at home. But today something has changed. What will it take for us to get it back again?

The assessments of Brooks, Putnam, and Edelman paint a bleak picture for the future of bad news kids. A bifurcation of American society, led by consumer-driven schooling, has taken its toll on the lives, families, and homes of many citizens. A whole class of people is being destroyed by their growing lack of opportunity to get ahead, even just a little bit.

One doesn't have to look too far to see this destruction. It can be seen each day in our large high schools where, as Alfie Kohn quoting David Labaree suggests,[5] our school system has been turned into a "vast public subsidy for private ambition," creating an arena filled with self-interested actors seeking opportunities for gaining educational distinctions at the expense of others. And the "others" are the bad news kids, who are paying a huge cost at being excluded from the opportunities available to the get-ahead, stay-ahead crowd.

Brooks's, Putnam's, and Edelman's assessments suggest these bad news kids and parents are the only ones being done in by our bifurcated schools. But there is more to the story. On the surface, the good news kids and their parents are the winners. However, they too are paying a huge cost in the system that they appear to rule. As Kohn suggests, for these students, everything has become about their future. The value of everything is solely a function of its contribution to the future, something that might come later.

They follow a path that will continue right through college, professional school, and into the early stages of a career, until at last "they wake up in a tastefully appointed bedroom to discover that their lives are mostly gone."[6] As noted in chapter 1, the parents of these high achievers have sacrificed their own children's present to the future. They are living a life basking in reflected glory. And their children often live in fear of letting their parents down.

The first step is to help educators, parents, and community members become aware of the cost of consumer-driven education to the entire school community. This awareness needs to ask the following questions.

- Whose school is it?
- If the school media promotions suggest there is an ongoing effort to provide equal opportunity for every student, then why isn't it happening?
- What opportunities are available for non–college bound students?
- What is the cost to high-achieving students and their parents who are being employed to market the success of their school?
- What is the cost to low-achieving students and their parents who are viewed as offering little good news and tokens to their school?
- What is the cost to the school principal, guidance counselors, and teachers in marketing good news students to demonstrate the school's success and pass budgets?

Finding ways to tell the truth through school community forums and dialogue might be a place to begin raising this awareness. This dialogue might offer its participants an opportunity to imagine their school in a new way with new designs. For example, they might imagine

- a school in which the good news kids are no longer used solely as "instruments of gain and objects of use" but are organized to come to the aid of bad news kids as team members. A process of helping others can have its own set of rewards and accolade. Knowing others, their lives and culture, can also be a powerful learning experience.
- a school in which the elite teachers of good news kids are organized to team with the teachers of bad news kids to share skills, resources, and learning activities.
- a school in which guidance counselors are organized to devote a fair share of their counseling services to bad news kids and parents, as well as to offer intervention for good news kids and parents around personal issues.
- a school in which the principal's role as chief marketer moves beyond simply marketing the stories of good news kids to now include stories/documentation of how long-held barriers are being removed by good news kids and their parents interacting and learning with/from bad news kids and their parents; of good news teachers and bad news teachers interacting and learning with/from each other; and of star guidance counselors, known as the "go-to persons" for college counseling, interacting and learning with/from counselors who are skilled in personal counseling and intervention.

These are examples of new designs that can help reduce the bifurcation in our schools that thrives on isolation and separation. They could lead to schools which are organized to be inclusive and to promote equal opportunity not only among students but also among parents, staff, and the administration, schools in which people of different backgrounds, social positions, abilities, and aspirations encounter one another in the course of everyday life and learn how to treat each other as worthy of dignity and respect.

NOTES

1. David Brooks, "The Opportunity Gap," www.nytimes.com/2012/07/10/opinion/brooks-the-opportunity-gap.html (accessed July 20, 2012).

2. David F. Labaree, *Someone Has to Fail: The Zero-Sum Game of Public Schooling* (Cambridge, MA: Harvard University Press, 2010).

3. Michael J. Sandel, *What Money Can't Buy: The Moral Limits on Money* (New York: Farrar, Straus and Giroux, 2012).

4. Marian Wright Edelman, "Pushing Children Out of School—A New American Value," www.huffingtonpost.com/marian-wright-edelman/pushing-children-out-of-s_b_1690870.html (accessed July 21, 2012).

5. Alfie Kohn, "Only for *My* Kid: How Privileged Parents Undermine School Reform," www.alfiekohn.org/teaching/ofmk.htm (accessed November 6, 2012).

6. Kohn, "Only for *My* Kid."

References

Brooks, David, "The Opportunity Gap," www.nytimes.com/2012/07/10/opinion/brooks-the-opportunity-gap.html (accessed July 20, 2012).

Brooks, Johney, "Marketing the Public Schools," *Education Leadership* (November 1982).

Brown, B., "Wellesley High Grads Told: You're Not Special," www.theswellesleyreport.com/2012/06/wellesley-high-grads-told-youre-not-special (accessed June 30, 2012).

Dunaway, David, "Myth of the SuperPrincipal," http://cnx.org/content/m20832/latest (accessed July 1, 2012).

Edelman, Marian Wright, "Pushing Children Out of School—A New American Value?" www.huffingtonpost.com/marian-wright-edelman/pushing-children-out-of-s_b_1690870.html(accessed July 21, 2012).

Education Trust, "Poised to Lead: How School Counselors Can Drive College and Career Readiness," *The Education Trust* (December 2011).

Fibkins, William L., "No Easy Way Out: Stories about American Adolescents," unpublished manuscript, 2006.

Friedman, Thomas L., "The Rise of Popularism," *New York Times*, June 24, 2012.

Inger, Morton, "Teacher Collaboration in Secondary Schools," http://vocserve.berkeley.edu/centerfocus/CF2.html (accessed July 3, 2012).

Kohn, Alfie, "Only for *My* Kid: How Privileged Parents Undermine School Reform," www.alfiekohn.org/teaching/ofmk.htm (accessed November 6, 2012).

Labaree, David F., *Someone Has to Fail: The Zero-Sum Game of Public Schooling* (Cambridge, MA: Harvard University Press, 2010).

Medina, Jennifer, "Pressed by Charters, Public Schools Try Marketing," www.nytimes.com/2010/03/10 (accessed June 20, 2012).

Public Agenda, "Rolling Up Their Sleeves: Superintendents and Principals Talk about What's Needed to Fix Public Schools," *Public Agenda* (2003).

Rehak, Melanie, "Things Fall Together," *New York Times*, March 26, 2000.

St. George, Donna, "College Comes to High School," www.washingtonpost.com/local/education/college-comes-to-high-school/2012/05/23/gJQAM8TrlU_story.html (accessed June 8, 2012).

Sandel, Michael J., *What Money Can't Buy: The Moral Limits of Money* (New York: Farrar, Straus and Giroux, 2012).

Schwarz, Alan, "In Their Own Words: 'Study Drugs,'" www.nytimes.com/interactive/2012/06/10/education/stimulants-student-voices.html (accessed June 11, 2012).

———, "Risky Rise of the Good Grade Pill," www.nytimes.com/2012/06/10/education/seeking-academic-edge-teenagers-abuse-stimulants.html?pagewanted=all (accessed June 11, 2012).

Sykes, Charles J., "No Rewards: The Attack on Excellence in America's Public Schools," http://my.execpc.com/-presswis/rewards.html (accessed June 8, 2012).

Virginia Beach City Public Schools, "Essential Tasks Principal, Senior High School," http://www.vbschools.com.hr/job-desc/principal%20hs.pdf (accessed July 8, 2012).

Warner, Judith, "Parents Created This Problem, and Must Address It," www.nytimes.com/roomfordebate/2012/06/09/fewer-prescriptions-for-adhd-less-drug-abuse/parents-have-fueled-the-abuse-of-adhd-medications (accessed June 10, 2012).

Winter, Gregg, "Wooing the Counselor Raises Enrollment and Also Eyebrows," *New York Times*, July 8, 2004.

About the Author

William L. Fibkins is an author and educational consultant specializing in training programs for school administrators, teachers, pupil service professionals, support staff, students, and parents. He holds degrees in school administration, counselor education, and health education from Syracuse University and the University of Massachusetts.